Diana,

For all the wise words of
Native American wisdom
that you've shared with me...
enjoy this reading & may
it be a part of your
path, your circle,
the beat of your drum,
your quest.

love you so,
Vickie

Native American
WISDOM

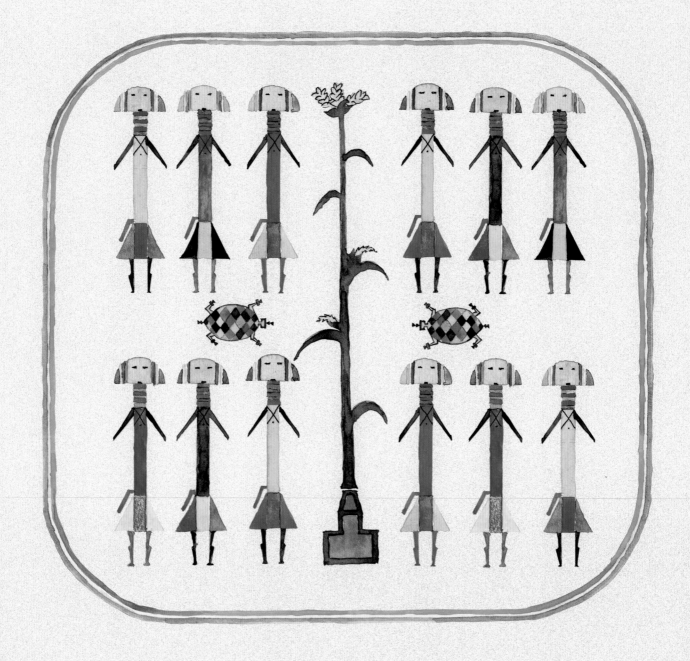

Native American
WISDOM

The Sacred in Everyday Life

CAMERON FLEET

BARNES
&NOBLE
BOOKS
NEW YORK

Author's note

Native American spirituality has as many forms as the number of First People, past and present, each of whose beliefs are unique. Some beliefs are common to the people of a band or tribe; others can be generalized for a culture area; and still other principles—albeit of the most abstract and general nature—can be said to hold for all Native Americans who have grown up in traditional communities or with an awareness of their cultural heritage. While this book cannot accurately reflect the beliefs of all Native Americans, nor of any particular group, the author hopes to convey some important aspects of the continent's indigenous spiritual life and has used "artistic license" in pursuit of this end. In order to emphasize the commonalities among the many different belief systems of today and generations past, I have combined words and images from a vast span of time and across all culture areas freely and according to my personal interpretations. I have generalized and ascribed particular beliefs more widely than they are actually held—perhaps, in some cases, contradicting or misrepresenting opinions and sacred traditions. For any such transgressions, I offer my apologies and assurance that no offense was intended.

During the course of the last several centuries, oral tradition has continued in an unbroken chain for many peoples, and this sometimes conflicts with written records documented by settlers, missionaries and anthropologists, each of whom transcribed speeches and reminiscences through the prism of his or her own beliefs and codes. Recently, the words of some well-known orators—including the legendary wisdom of Chief Seathl—have been rewritten from their previously accepted translations as a result of much important scholarship. The editors and I have worked together in selecting and phrasing quotations and proverbs that are often recorded in a number of different versions. We have attributed these to the individual and tribe names that are most widely known today, rather than adopting the names chosen by people for themselves and their ancestors, for the purposes of accessibility to a general readership. In some cases, we have retold legends and simplified complex myths and tales, as my mother, a Cherokee, retold stories for me and my sisters and brother. It is our hope that the reader will accept these liberties and enjoy this celebration of Native American wisdom, of the sacred in everyday life.

—CAMERON FLEET

FOR CATHY DOLAN, A WONDERFUL FRIEND

This edition published by Barnes and Noble, Inc., by arrangement with Saraband Inc.

2000 Barnes & Noble Books

Copyright © 2000 Saraband Inc

Design © Ziga Design

Library of Congress Cataloging in Publication Data available

ISBN: 0-7607-1379-0

Printed in China

10 9 8 7 6 5 4 3 2 1

Contents

Introduction: This Sacred Land

When I was ten years of age I looked at the land and the rivers, the sky above, and the animals around me and could not fail to realize that they were made by some great power.

—BRAVE BUFFALO, SIOUX

North America rests between and along the arms of two great mountain ranges: the high mountains of the West reaching south from Alaska all the way to Central America, and the lesser heights of the Appalachians in the East extending from Georgia to Maine. Between these ranges vast lands spread far north from the hot, arid region of northern Mexico, across prairie lands and majestic alluvial plains veined by the Mississippi River and its great tributaries, to the pine-forested marshland taiga of Canada and beyond, to the tundra bordering the icy shores of the Arctic Ocean.

The eastern slopes of the timeworn Appalachian Mountains fall away into the foothills of piedmont country and the Atlantic coastal littoral. Its western slopes dwindle into hills and prairie lands that extend to the Great Plains. Northeast of these plains, enormous glaciers once scoured the landscape to form the Great Lakes and the Hudson Bay. Between the northwestern Great Plains and the mountains of the Pacific coast, a high plateau reaches down from Canada to northern Oregon, Idaho and western Montana. South of this region, mountains enclose the arid lands of the Great Basin, which descend to the plateau country and deserts of the North American Southwest.

Such is the shape of the great North American continent: its mountains, hills and valleys; its high plateau, great basin and southwestern desert; its prairies and vast plains; its great rivers and lakes and streams; the once-endless forests of the East and the subtropical regions of southern California and Florida.

This is the living and sacred land of Native America.

Before people lived on this sacred land, the continent was an Eden that had evolved freely for millions of years. For eons the seasons had turned in their cycles, the grasses had sung in the wind, the waters had sparkled in the light of the rising sun and had turned to fire at sunset. For millennia the streams, lakes and rivers had teemed with fish, birds had soared into the sky and sung in the branches of flowering trees, and many kinds of animals had flourished in the rich and complex ecologies of the virgin continent. The land belonged to these creatures and they belonged

to the land. This had been so for a time as timeless as the morning sun and the distant stars that burned in the night skies over the vast wilderness, as timeless as the moon, the thunder, the rain and the wind.

Then humanity came into this land, and as the first people moved across the continent in pursuit of game and other sustenance, they felt reverence for the living land and all of its life forms. Surely, sickness and hunger, suffering and hardship, failure and disappointment were not unknown to them. They wondered at the causes of these things and sought their remedies. They knew death, and feared sickness. They felt gratitude and joy for the generosity of the Earth. As the seasons continued to turn, the newcomers spiraled across the continent and increased. Game was abundant, and the land was a garden to the people. They found many edible and useful roots, plants and fruits. As generation succeeded generation, for a thousand generations and more, they learned the lore of the animals

and the plants, and as their reverence for the Earth deepened, so they grew in the wisdom of the land. For everything was one, and they were one with everything. And they are still among us, for their life is in this land.

At the time of European discovery, the native peoples were scattered throughout North America. Some lived in permanent villages, tending crops; some were nomadic, hunting and gathering as they moved; still others had seasonal homes, gathering resources and preserving foods during the busy summer months, then settling down in protected lodges for the harsh winter. These peoples spoke a richly diverse range of hundreds of distinct languages, many of which may be associated with six major linguistic families: Eskimo-Aleut, Algonquian-Wakashan, Na-Dené, Penutian, Hokan-Siouan and Aztec-Tanoan. Despite the pronounced differences in lifeways and beliefs that spanned the continent at this time, the common links among the peoples were strong. Perhaps they were once one family, whose descendants had migrated along paths reflected in their language patterns. But few myths and legends speak of migration: Most believed that they had been born into the land that they occupied.

All tribes possessed an oral literature of myths and legends. These stories embodied their ancestral memories and formed the foundations of their culture. These myths, tales and stories, whose transmission to the generations was entrusted to holy people and wise elders with gifted memories, express wisdom and spirituality developed over countless generations. Many of them have been preserved to this day and have recurred, in whole or in part, in various versions throughout North America. They offer an entrance to the wisdom of a heritage that still lives among us. But we must remember that the tales themselves are not the living wisdom. They served to show the way to it.

Native Americans generally lived in clan groups of families, rarely more than a band or village of closely related

Left: Maidens Sing for the Streams of Life, *a contemporary painting by Jesse Hummingbird with traditional symbols including the four directions, feather fans and headdresses and the zigzag red bands of the universal streams of life.*

Previous pages: A Zuñi village dwarfed by the monumental cliffs that rise abruptly from the New Mexican landscape.

Pages 6-7: Sunset over the Blue Ridge Mountains, Virginia.

souls. These groups often shared a tribal identity with their neighbors, and the tribes themselves would sometimes form intertribal confederacies. Most small groups joined in large gatherings at certain times of the year for feasts and ceremonies. While most bands and villages were small, some settlements, especially in the East, might count up to 1,000 inhabitants. Among the Cherokee and other tribes of the Southeast, the populations of some larger villages exceeded 2,000. Although many tribes practiced a seminomadic hunting and gathering existence, before the introduction of the horse and the disturbance of their villages by the arrival of Europeans, most Native American communities were settled in relatively small territories that their inhabitants knew intimately.

Indeed, this knowledge of the land and its ways was at once the most immediate and the most inclusive truth of identity and belonging in relationship with all the living spirits of creation, from Mother Earth to the overarching presence of Father Sky. Native Americans lived in union with the Earth, which they revered almost universally as their mother. They were of the Earth and it was from the Earth that they and all living creatures drew their substance and their sustenance, both materially and spiritually. This reverence for the Mother and for the Earth, this identification of all living things as being of

the same family, this mystic sense of oneness was at the heart of Indian life and spirituality. Native Americans lived in a world of spirit. Everything around them was alive. They hunted with reverence for the spirit of their prey. They gathered and cultivated sacred plants with reverence for the gifts of the Earth. They related tales of their sacred origins and of all the shapes and spirits of life that surrounded them, had preceded them and would follow them and succeeding generations.

The customs, lifeways and traditions of the tribes of Native America were shaped by the varying conditions of

Overleaf: A Lakota mother and child pose against pictographs of their ancestral way of life, which was becoming a memory in 1891, when this photograph was taken.

Right: A Tsuu T'ina woman of the Canadian Plains dries food over a fire to preserve it.

life in the ten diverse regions of the continent: the Arctic coasts and tundra, the Subarctic taiga, the Great Plains, the Woodlands of the Northeast and the Southeast, the Northwest Coast, California, the Great Plateau, the Great Basin and the Southwest. Although their expression of beliefs and practices varied, the native peoples shared many of them, held also by tribal peoples throughout the world.

Above all, they lived in profound identification and relationship with the living land and all its creatures. The "boundary" between the human and the natural worlds was permeable and mediated by powerful spirits representing all the phenomena of nature. Human beings did not place themselves above nature. They were part of it, respectful and dependent upon it. Through direct spiritual communion with the natural world, they could partake of its powers.

Hunting peoples asked forgiveness of their prey and observed a host of taboos to avoid the danger of offending them. Animals were objects of respect and gratitude. Their meat provided nourishment; their fur and skins provided clothing and shelter; their very bones and sinews provided material for any number of tools. Most hunters believed that animals voluntarily offered their bodies for the kill. Indeed, many tribal stories reflect the view that animals created the world and had a place in it before humankind. Animals were worshipped for the beauty of their adaptation to the integrity of the environment. They were often regarded as superior to humans in intelligence and cunning and as emblems of speed and power. And they were also endowed with the full panoply of the best moral qualities—and some of the worst as well. People patterned themselves on totemic animals and sought their power to ensure human survival in the natural world.

Since everything could be invested with the power of spirit, native peoples made use of many amulets and totems. They sought the protection of these objects and preserved them carefully in sacred bundles. Their power could aid an individual or group in any of life's challenges. These objects had the power to bring good fortune in many forms. They could cure sickness, ensure good weather or success in the hunt. Often the power of these amulets was directly associated with their nature. Thus a necklace of bear claws brought to the wearer the strength and courage of a bear,

or a garment of eagle feathers the freedom and speed of an eagle's flight. Sometimes these objects had become powerful through some past success attributed to them. Thus a crystal that had been used successfully in a healing rite could be used again to the same effect. These amulets and totems were often passed down from one generation to the next, binding the generations each to the other. Above all, they bound the people in close relation to the natural world: This bond was the real magic of any object that became a focus of reverence.

The men of many tribes sought the power of the world of animals and spirits in their dreams and their quests for visions. But the women were perceived as possessing the great powers of creating life within themselves. Men respected and feared this power. Women were closely identified with the Earth that was the mother of all creation and the source of all sustenance. And just as men knew that they were born of the Earth, they knew that to the Earth they must return in death. This dark power of generativity was held in awe. Menstruation was a rite of passage surrounded by ceremonies and taboos across the continent. The fertile powers of women were both worshipped and dreaded.

Native Americans looked to those among them who were gifted to commune with the natural world, who had special powers, taught or conferred upon them through their privileged contact with the supernatural. These shamans and medicine men were among the natural leaders of the hunting communities. Where native societies evolved into more stable communities based on agriculture, the pre-eminent role of the shaman was often assumed by a priestly class of male and female leaders who were responsible for the ceremonies and rituals that ensured economic and political order.

This book is a dream of spirit and religion shared by all the first peoples of the diverse regions of the North American continent. This spirit is alive in the memory of the landscape and in our memory of all who breathed and dreamed and walked upon it before our present day. This spirit of Native America is alive to us and can enrich the lives of all among us who reach for its treasures. So let us venture as eagles in flight into the mystic wealth of the spirit of Native America.

Creation and the World

Earth and stones fell down from the sky to form the land. Babies were born out of this earth and grew up among the young willows. A man and a woman appeared; the woman made clothes for the children and the man brought food to them. The man stamped upon the earth and dogs sprang forth. In the beginning there was neither death nor sunlight. An old woman said, "Let us be without light, if so we can be without death," but another said, "No! Let us have both light and death." And as she spoke, it was so.

—ARCTIC CREATION STORY

Creation is ongoing.

—LAKOTA PROVERB

Throughout North America, parents, elders and wisdom keepers have long recited the creation stories and wisdom traditions of their tribes to members gathered around campfires or in lodges. Traditionally, these gatherings were often held in the winter, especially during the winter solstice, when they had a magical function: Their incantation marked the turning of the annual cycle to the lengthening days and the rebirth of spring. Re-enactments of the world's creation, ceremonial recitations of ancestral folkways, ensured the continuation of the nurturing world and its many life forms. Such recitations often included sacred songs known to only a few.

Passed unchanged through oral tradition across the generations, the ancient songs held ritual power and wisdom. In telling and retelling these stories about the creation of the world, important lessons on the nature of the world—the universe itself and all its living creatures— and on how people should live and behave were passed down through the generations.

Creation stories occur with both common elements and wide variations across the North American continent. Many tribes, including the Cherokee, believed that the upper world of the sky and the lower world of the primeval sea had existed long before the creation of the Earth, and that the birds and beasts, once as crowded in the heavens as the stars, had dreamt of a more spacious world in which to live.

Often the Earth was created by a female figure, underlining the importance of the mother's role and her association with the Earth itself. In this Mohegan creation story, the first woman descended from the sky:

At first there was nothing but sea and sky.
Then a woman floated down from the sky.
As she touched down, a point of land rose out of the water
and became a little island.
Here the woman became First Mother and gave birth to
three beings: Bear, Wolf and Deer. The First Mother then
returned to the sky. The little island spread and stretched
itself into a mainland, and Bear, Wolf and Deer became the
ancestors of all life.

—MOHEGAN BELIEF

Previous pages: *Pictographs (rock paintings) of a prehistoric creation story made by long-vanished inhabitants of Utah at what is now Canyonlands National Park.*

Opposite: *A contemporary acrylic painting by Jesse Hummingbird depicting a wolf dancer preparing to compete in a "fancy dance" against his brother, costumed as the powerful bear totem:* Wolf Dances Fancy.

Left: Winter Hunters, *by Kiowa/Comanche artist Barthell Little Chief, is a powerful evocation of the Plains warrior's unity with nature, personified by the sacred buffalo, source of food, clothing and shelter.*

Overleaf: *Hopi Kachina dolls, used to teach Pueblo children about the cloud spirits invoked by ritual dancers to bring prosperity, fertility, rain and other gifts to the community.*

I shall always live in my children, and my children's children.

— NEW CORN, POTOWATOMI

In some traditions, people existed before the world was created: These ancestors had a hand in bringing their world into being. Such stories serve to remind people that their actions carry consequences for others, even for those yet unborn, and that the ancestors must be remembered and respected. Inuit peoples told that the sun and moon were once mortals. Unlike most traditions, the Inuit believe that the sun is female and the moon, male. They were created in this way:

Under cover of darkness, a girl was visited by an unknown lover. Wishing to know his identity, when the lover returned, the girl stroked his face with cinders from the dead embers of a fire. Later, she saw that it was her brother's face that was streaked with ash, and she was furious. In anger she seized a flaming torch and pursued him as he fled from her, ashamed. She followed him all the way into the heavens. As they rose into the sky the sister's torch burned ever more brightly, and she became the sun, creating stars as sparks flew from her torch. The man changed into the moon: he remains in darkness to this day as he flees from the wrath of his fiery sister.

— INUIT CREATION STORY

In the creation story of Taos Pueblo, too, the first people formed the world:

The boy cried and cried. The blood came out, and finally he died. With his tears our lakes became. With his blood the red clay became. With his body our mountains became, and that was how the Earth became.

— TAOS PUEBLO CREATION STORY

The fish and the game are the essence of my life. I was not brought here from a foreign country and did not come here. I was put here by the creator.

— MENINOCK, YAKIMA

Many native peoples believed that the Earth was created when a diving animal scooped a small portion of mud or a grain of sand from the depths of the primeval sea. From this small beginning, the earth magically expanded, often supported on the back of an animal like the turtle, whose shell symbolized the vault of heaven joined to the Earth. The peoples who sprang from an earth created or supported by animals must forever remember their interdependence on, and indebtedness to, the animals who share their world. According to Iroquois legend:

In the heavens long ago, a stately tree ever blossoming and bearing fruit scented the air with its flowers. The Great Ruler and his people gathered in council beneath this tall tree. One day a vast sea cloud called for light, and the Great Ruler ordered that the tree be uprooted. Summoning the pregnant Ata-en-sic, or Sky Mother, he wrapped her in light and sent her down to the sea cloud.

Alarmed by the approaching brilliance, the birds and the other animals took council.

"Where can it rest?" the Duck cried.

"Only the oeh-da (earth) that lies beneath the waters can hold it," replied Beaver, who tried to gather the oeh-da but did not return.

Duck, too, tried but his body floated dead upon the surface of the waters. Others tried but failed, until muskrat returned with a small portion in his paw.

"It is heavy and it will grow fast," muskrat explained, "But who will bear it?"

Turtle volunteered, and the oeh-da was placed upon its shell.

— IROQUOIS CREATION STORY

Opposite: The turtle is a widespread symbol of both creation and endurance, its shell representing the meeting of earth and sky, as well as a protective barrier against spiritual and physical danger.

Below: Stars, plants, animals, ancestral spirits and abstract symbols are incorporated in these traditional Southwestern basket designs.

columns that touched it at the sacred cardinal points. In other belief systems, the world was supported by a central pillar, or a tree. The arc of the rising and setting sun divided the central plane into the cardinal points of east, west, north and south, which were home to the four winds and the great powers upholding the world.

The four cardinal directions and the three levels of sky, earth, and underworld formed a world in seven dimensions, the whole of which was regarded as a living organism that nourished all life—animals, birds, fish, plants and humankind. Four and seven became sacred numbers in many tribal traditions. With wide variations from region to region and from tribe to tribe, each of the world's four quarters might be associated with a symbolic color, opening the way to complex systems of color symbolism for objects and creatures of all kinds—shells, stones, feathers, flowers, birds, animals, maize—which were in turn associated with the cardinal points.

The order and intricacy of the spider's web was widely seen as a metaphor for the interrelatedness of all creation, and this image often occurs as an artistic motif. The spider spins its web from its own body, the filaments radiating outward from the center. A symbol of the spider's crucial role in the discovery of the sacred fire, the cross represents the world and its four cardinal points. At the center of the cross, set in the circle of the world, is the sacred fire:

ometimes the first people arose from the Earth fully formed. In the Southwest, the Navajo and some of the Pueblo peoples believed that the world emerged in evolutionary stages from subterranean darkness, as seen in the ceremonials performed by the Hopi, Zuñi and Navajo. With each stage, people learned and grew until they became fully evolved inhabitants of the present world.

As beliefs evolved through the millennia, many native peoples of North America came to perceive the earth as an island suspended from the heavens by four cords or

At night the created world was often cold. The moon shed no warmth and the creatures of the world appealed to heaven for the warming agent of fire, which was sent to them in the form of lightning. But no living creature could collect this gift, though many, like the raven and the black snake, tried and were scorched and marked by it. Finally, the spider wove a special basket in which the ember could be held and carried.

—CHEROKEE TRADITION

When the wisdom keepers speak, all should listen.

—SENECA

*The Great Spirit sees
and hears everything,
and never forgets.*

—CHIEF JOSEPH, NEZ PERCÉ

The idea of a supreme creative being was central to some peoples, this being generally expressed as the great mystery of the totality of creation rather than articulated as its agent. Exceptions included the Blackfoot belief in the personal creator known as Na'pi, or Old Man, and the Salish cycle, as expressed in this traditional story of the Snohomish creator Dohkwibuhch, or Changer:

Changer made the world, starting in the East and moving West, creating groups of people and giving each its own language. As he made his way across the world, he made the animals and the trees and the sky. But Changer made the sky so low that some of the people and animals stumbled into the Sky World. All the peoples, with the help of their animals, worked together to push up the sky. When the sky was raised, three hunters, their dog and an elk were trapped above; they became the Big Dipper.

—SNOHOMISH CREATION STORY

The tribes of the American Southeast spoke of the Great Flame of Being. Those of the Great Plains referred to a Great Spirit or Great Mystery dwelling beyond the arch of the remote and shining sky. The breath of life and the light that revealed creation were manifestations of this transcendent power. As the "Breath of Life," it was manifested in the movement of the winds. As the "Spirit of Light," the supreme being was revealed in the sun, "the Eye of the Great Spirit." Some peoples taught that the world had been willed into existence by a shadowy great creator—even that this creator had made the world from

his or her own body. But in most cases, the supreme being remained aloof from the work of creating humanity and the world. These tasks were left to lesser beings.

Hosts of demi-gods, heavenly bodies, and animal and human figures endowed with supernatural powers played a part in nature, like the Four Beneficial Spirits of the Potowatomi, who believed that:

Manibozho placed four beneficial spirits at the four cardinal points of the earth, for the purpose of contributing to the happiness of the human race. That of the north procures for us ice and snow, in order to aid us in discovering and following the wild animals. That of the south gives us that which occasions the growth of our pumpkins, melons, maize, and tobacco. The spirit placed at the west gives us rain, and that of the east gives us light, and commands the sun to make his daily walks around the globe.

—POTOGOJECS, POTOWATOMI

Overleaf: *Coyote, a culture hero variously revered and feared as he goes his solitary way by night (left).*

Spectacular monuments carved by Nature herself at Arches National Park, Utah (right).

Old Man's Story

Na'pi, Old Man, made all things, and all things knew him and spoke with him—birds, animals and man and woman. Old Man gave them laws. Old Man came from the south, and as he traveled north he formed mountains and plains, trees and rivers. It was he who painted the landscape as we see it today. In the plains he set a place to grow camas, berries, wild carrots, turnips and sweet and bitter roots. He created the bighorn sheep for the mountains, where they skip fearlessly among the rocks, while the graceful antelope were made to speed across the prairies.

Na'pi took clay to make a woman and her child. "You must be people," he said as he formed them into human shape. Then he covered the clay and went away. The next morning he saw the shapes had changed a little. Each day more changes took place, until the fourth morning, when he told the images to rise and walk and they went to the river with their Maker.

"Will this go on forever? Will we always live?" the woman asked as they stood by the river.

"I have never thought of that," Na'pi said, "We must decide by throwing this buffalo chip into the water. If it floats, people will come alive again after only four days. But if it sinks to the bottom, there will be an end to them."

Old Man threw the chip into the river and it floated. "No," the woman said picking up a stone, "If this stone floats we will always live. But if it sinks people must die so that they will always be sorry for one another."

The woman threw the stone into the water and watched as it sank.

"There," said the Old Man, "You have chosen." Not long afterward the child died and the woman wept sadly.

"Let us change the law to the first law you made," the woman said.

"We will undo nothing. People will have to die," Old Man said.

Na'pi took the first people through forests and marsh lands and across the prairies, showing them the fruits of the land. They were poor and naked, and he taught them to hunt and eat the flesh of birds and animals and instructed them in the healing power of all herbs.

As he continued north he created more people and the buffalo who would provide their food. He showed them how to hunt with a bow and arrow, and the people prospered and became numerous. Old Man said, "Sleep if you are tired, for you will gain strength and your dreams will help you. You must obey the animals that appear in your dreams, for they shall be your guide. If you cry aloud an eagle, a buffalo or perhaps a bear may answer your prayer and you must listen." And so first people lived by the power of dreams.

As Old Man journeyed north he created many more people, leaving his form near Red Deer's River where he slept, and on a high hill where he found a fine hiding place. In time he stopped and marked off a piece of ground.

"This is your land," he said to the five tribes— Blackfoot, Sarcee, Piegan, Gros Ventre and Blood. "Let no other people come here. If strangers cross this line, take your bows and arrows and give them battle. For if they gain a footing in this land trouble will come to you."

Our ancestors fought all who crossed these lines and kept them out. In recent times, the white people came, and you know what happened when we failed to obey the Old Man's laws.

—Blackfoot Creation Story

Be kind to everything that lives.

—OMAHA PROVERB

any traditions told of "culture heroes," half-animal, half-human beings, who were born to shape the newly created world, to bring laws and to teach the people the arts of living. These heroes quelled hideous beings that often took the forms of serpents and water monsters. Sometimes twin heroes—one representing good, the other evil—struggled with each other for mastery of the world. Good prevailed, and the evil spirit was banished.

Coyote and Raven, "tricksters," or culture heroes endowed with supernatural powers, played a role in many creation myths. The oral literature of Coyote, the most common of these figures, often portrayed him as the companion of a paternal creator who sometimes banished him from the scene because he was so destructive. Although he could be kind, the trickster Coyote was often malevolent. His fateful, often unwise, decisions explained why life was as it was.

In the Pacific Northwest, several tribes believe that the shape-shifter Raven helped create the animals and fish by bringing daylight to the world. A Tlingit story tells that:

Once the world was completely dark. The sun, moon and stars were kept in three wooden boxes that were guarded by a chief. Raven wanted to bring sunlight to the people and sought a way to get hold of the chief's precious boxes. He turned himself into a splinter of hemlock, which the chief's daughter ate. She then gave birth to a child, Raven. The boy played, slowly winning his grandfather's affections. One day he convinced the chief to let him play with the wooden boxes. He pulled them open and flung the stars and moon across the sky. Then he changed back into a bird and flew away with the sun, bringing it back to his people.

—TLINGIT LEGEND

The often comic misdeeds of the mercurial "trickster" were not only a source of laughter, but also of cautionary instruction in the consequences of careless or evil behavior for the community. Such tales warned of the dangers of disobedience to higher authority and violations of the web of life.

The myths of creation have always been told with reverence for all life. They help to explain or express the world's existence: how it came to be. Even more importantly, they have a restorative ritual function: to maintain the world in its established cyclical order of sustaining life, of rising and setting suns and moons, of rotating stars and constellations, of revolving seasons, of cycles of birth, death and renewal.

Spirit, Power and Nature

All life is wakan. So also is everything which exhibits power, whether in action, as the winds and drifting clouds, or in passive endurance, as the boulder by the wayside. For even the commonest sticks and stones have a spiritual essence which must be reverenced as a manifestation of the all-pervading mysterious power that fills the universe.

—OSAGE

Nature is filled with unseen, mysterious and pervasive supernatural forces, according to Native American belief. Experiencing everything in the world as alive and constantly interacting, a host of potent spirit beings were personified and venerated: spirits found in the sun and the moon; in animals and birds and all living creatures; in stone and wood and in all forms of matter; in thunder, wind, rain and all natural phenomena. Each of these entities possessed power great or small by which it maintained its form and being and affected the form and being of everything around it. In the words of Black Elk:

We regard all created beings as sacred and important, for everything has a wochangi, or influence, which can be given to us, through which we may gain a little more understanding if we are attentive. We should understand well that all things are the works of the Great Spirit. We should know that He is within all things; the trees, the grasses, the rivers, the mountains and all the four-legged animals, and the winged peoples; and even more important, we should understand that He is also above all these things and peoples.

— BLACK ELK, LAKOTA

All plants are our brothers and sisters. They talk to us, and if we listen carefully, we can hear them.

— ARAPAHO BELIEF

Previous pages: *Glacial peaks ring remote Hector Lake, in Alberta, Canada.*

These pages: *A Kutenai duck hunter slips through the reeds in search of game in this serene photograph by Edward S. Curtis.*

Native peoples gave various names to this all-pervasive power. The Inuit referred to it as *Inua* or "owner." Siouan peoples knew it as *Wakan*. For the Huron it was *Oki*; Algonquian peoples called it *Manitou*, or *Manito*, or *Manido*. The Iroquois called it *Orenda*, or, when it was an evil power, *Otgon*. The Iroquois believed that all individual beings — plants, animals, men and spirits — possessed *orenda* in various degrees. The "Earth Grasper" of Iroquois mythology possessed supreme powers of *orenda* and could not be harmed. The little otter possessed very little *orenda* and was vulnerable.

Although the simplest meaning of all these terms is power, they can also be translated as magic, mystery, wonder, or spirit, for they signified all of these things. The power could be common and slight or, increasing through the orders of creation, could have enormous force and

assume the complex forms of intelligent spirits who could hear and respond to supplications. Wherever they could be applied to the needs of humanity, these powers were thought of as medicine, both spiritual and physical.

The continuity that prevailed across the spectrum of life is expressed in this traditional story:

> *A worm is eaten by a bird. Then the bird is eaten by a cat whose self-satisfaction is disrupted by a mean-looking dog. After devouring the cat, the dog is killed by a grizzly bear. [Then] comes a man who kills the bear and climbs a mountain to proclaim his superiority. He ran so hard up the mountain that he collapsed and died at the top. Before long, the worm crawled out of his body.*

> —CHUMASH LEGEND

The supernatural and the magical permeated every aspect of Native American life, and shaped its cultures and institutions. Reflecting an acute awareness of the delicate balance between humankind and nature, native peoples were and are sensitive to the rich variety of spirit powers. Exerting forces for either good or evil, all of these powers had to be propitiated. Well-being depended on harnessing such powers to ensure favorable weather conditions, good hunting and fishing, or abundant crops. Illnesses were often cured through the magical aid of supernatural powers. Magic provided protection from hostile forces and could be used to punish the transgressions of others.

Some special characteristic of an object or creature would often reveal its unique power to the careful observer. It might also be understood through experience, or revealed in a dream or a vision. Powerful objects were "good medicine," which strengthened those who possessed them. People sought contact with the spirit world to acquire these powers and their totemic objects, and the spirit world sought individuals upon whom to bestow power. A Great Plains shaman described his people's perceptions in terms of *wakan*:

> *Every object in the world has a spirit, and that spirit is* wakan. *Thus the spirit of the tree or things of that kind are also* wakan....*These* wakan *beings are greater than mankind in the same way that mankind is greater than animals. They can do many things that mankind cannot do. Mankind can pray to the* wakan *beings for help.*
>
> — LAKOTA BELIEF

We are all one child, spinning through Mother Sky.

— SHAWNEE

Opposite: Brothers of the Night, *by Kiowa/Comanche artist Barthell Little Chief, who says: "The owl is a creature of the earth and a brother.... If its message is one of death or misfortune, you will know it in your heart when you see the owl. In this painting, the owl is with the man as a brother of the night."*

When we show
our respect for
other living things,
they respond with
respect for us.
— ARAPAHO PROVERB

ust as native peoples valued peace and harmony within their tribes and confederations, they understood the importance of living in respectful harmony with the natural world:

Every part of the soil is sacred in the estimation of my people. Every hillside, every valley, every plain and grove, has been hallowed by some sad or happy event in days long vanished. Even the rocks, which seem to be dumb and dead as they swelter in the sun along the silent shore, thrill with memories of stirring events connected with the lives of my people, and the very dust on which you now stand responds more lovingly to their footsteps than to yours, because it is rich with the blood of our ancestors and our bare feet are conscious of the sympathetic touch.

— CHIEF SEATHL

Native American myths and legends may be seen as a partial, sometimes shattered, record of the dance of the spirit powers that brought the world into being and determined its shape, its nature and the course of its development. This dance is one of constant interaction among a host of forces personified in nature, sometimes assuming half-human, half-animal forms, which variously bestowed blessings on humanity and cursed it with calamities and mortality. As a Northwest Coast spokesman expressed this interdependence:

We felt that all things were like us people, down to small animals like the mouse, and the things like wood. The wood is glad to the person who is using it, and the person is glad to the wood for being there to be used.

— YUPIK TRADITION

Opposite: *Curtis's compelling portrait of the Oglala Sioux Slow Bull,* entitled Prayer to the Great Mystery.

Below: Woodlands Women, *by Cherokee artist Jeanne Walker Rorex, who says of this painting: "Two women, two friends, gathering wood for the next morning's fire. The sharing of stories…, smiles…and work were a way of life."*

The supreme law of the land is the Great Spirit's law, not man's law.

—HOPI

Opposite: *An Ojibwa tipi seems part of the landscape — a northern aspen grove — in this Curtis photograph of a summer encampment.*

Some native peoples believed in a supreme spirit whose unifying power radiated throughout creation. Generally envisioned as residing beyond the perceived world, this spirit, the great mystery and source of all, dwelt in everything and was beyond comprehension. Father Sky, often symbolized by the vault of heaven, was venerated, as was the sun, with its omniscient view of all matters occurring under its gaze, and such heavenly bodies as the moon and the morning star. In the realm of the skies dwelt the powers of the clouds and the four winds, of tempests and the rains. Among the great powers in this domain were the Eagle, the Hawk and the great Thunderbird, whose eyes flashed lightning and whose wings produced claps of thunder.

Fire, fog, rainfall, mists and the four directions were venerated, as were mountains and rivers and other features of the landscape. Mother Earth was recognized as a supreme power. Powerful animal spirits—Animal Elders or Guardians—filled the world with game and came to the aid of the hunter. Hosts of other powers swarmed upon and beneath the Earth.

When the north wind blows strong, the Bear is prowling in the sky; if the west wind is violent, the Panther is whining; when the east wind blows chill with its rain, the Moose is spreading its breath; when the south wind wafts breezes, the Fawn is returning to its Doe.

—IROQUOIS BELIEF

The idea of a supreme being was widespread, not only among the structured agricultural societies, but among those Plains peoples who became nomadic after acquiring horses. Some Southeastern tribes believed in a supreme being called the "Master of Breath." This ultimate being, whose earthly aspect was fire, was often associated with the sun, and its worship was conducted mainly by a priestly caste: The average person felt closer to the many lesser spirits that affected his or her daily life.

The Algonquians of the North recognized Gitche (or Kitshi) Manito, the Great Spirit, as the most important of their Manitos. They also called him the Master of Life. Invisible and immaterial, a source of great good to humanity, Gitche Manito had no fixed form or personality. He was the Great Mystery, the Great Unknown who was the source of all creation. Such a supreme being was known by other names among other peoples. The missionary Père Le Jeune, writing in 1633 of the Montagnais, records: "They say that there is a certain one whom they call *Atahocan*, who made all things." A similar Great Spirit, called *Kiehtan*, was recognized by the peoples of Massachusetts. The native people of Virginia told early Europeans of their belief in "one chiefe God that hath beene from all eternitie."

Wakan Tanka's Gifts

All living creatures and all plants derive their life from the sun. If it were not for the sun, there would be darkness and nothing could grow—the earth would be without life. Yet the sun must have the help of the earth. If the sun alone were to act on animals and plants, the heat would be so great that they would die, but there are clouds that bring rain, and the action of the sun and the earth together supply the moisture that is needed for life. The roots of a plant go down, and the deeper they go, the more moisture they find. This is according to the laws of nature and is one of the evidences of the wisdom of Wakan tanka. Plants are sent by Wakan tanka and come from the ground at his command, the part to be affected by the sun and the rain appearing above the ground and the roots pressing downward to find the moisture which is supplied for them.

Animals and plants are taught by Wakan tanka what they are to do. Wakan tanka teaches the birds to make nests, yet the nests of all birds are not alike. Wakan tanka gives them merely the outline. Some make better nests than others. In the same way, some animals are satisfied with very rough dwellings, while others make attractive places in which to live. Some animals also take better care of their young than others. The forest is the home of many birds and other animals, and the water is the home of fish and reptiles. All birds, even those of the same species, are not alike, and it is the same with animals and with human beings. The reason Wakan tanka does not make two birds, or animals, or human beings exactly alike is because each is placed here by Wakan tanka to be an independent individuality and to rely on itself. Some animals are made to live on the ground. The stones and the minerals are placed in the ground by Wakan tanka, some stones being more exposed than others. When a medicine man says he talks with the sacred stones, it is because of all the substances in the ground, these are the ones which most often appear in dreams and are able to communicate with men.

From my boyhood I have observed leaves, trees and grass, and I have never found two alike. They may have a general likeness, but on examination I have found that they differ slightly. Plants are of different families....It is the same with animals....It is the same with human beings; there is some place which is best adapted to each. The seeds of the plants are blown about by the wind until they reach the place where they will grow best—where the action of the sun and the presence of moisture are most favorable to them, and there they take root and grow. All living creatures and all plants are a benefit to something. Certain animals fulfill their purpose by definite acts. The crows, buzzards and flies are somewhat similar in their use, and even the snakes have purpose in being. In the early days the animals probably roamed over a very wide country until they found a proper place. An animal depends a great deal on the natural conditions surrounding it.

—Okute [Shooter], Teton Sioux

Right: The Berry Gatherers *by Curtis shows* women harvesting the bounties of nature, as they have done across the continent, whether on seasonal migrations or in the vicinity of settled villages.

The Realm of the Skies

We are the stars that sing,

We sing with our light

We are the birds of fire,

We fly over the sky.

We look down on the mountains

This is the song of the stars.

— ALGONQUIAN POEM

By day and night, the impact of the sky—the domain of the sun, moon, stars and weather—is deeply felt on the Earth and by all its living creatures. Both sun and moon were widely regarded as created beings, with the sun sometimes described as the Eye of the Great Spirit. Where hunting dominated as a way of life, in the forests of the Northeast and on the Great Plains, the sun was sometimes revered as a being under the domain of a greater sky god. Among agricultural peoples, whose survival depended upon the cyclic order of the sun and the seasons, sun worship often had pre-eminence. This was particularly true of the peoples of the Southeast.

In the Southwest and on the Northwest Coast, many perceived the sun and moon as material objects that were carried across the heavens. The moon was regarded as a powerful, often a dangerous, spirit. In most cases, the sun was identified as masculine and the moon as feminine.

The Iroquois say that the powerful Sun, Adekagagwaa, rests in the southern skies during the winter season, leaving his "sleep spirit" to keep watch in his place. Before his departure, he addresses the earth and its creatures, promising to return to still the howling winds, quiet the thunder and drive away winter and the raging storms.

Pueblo stories about the creation of the heavenly bodies reflect Southwestern beliefs about the pre-existence of the First People in a lower world and their passage to the world we know. A Zia legend describes the star-making sisters Ut'set and Now'utset, respectively the mothers of the native peoples and all others:

When the star people lived in the lower world, they formed beautiful groups and were not scattered across the sky as they now are. When the people were ready to pass to the upper world, Ut'set called the mole and told him to go first, with the sackful of stars. Not knowing what he carried, the mole soon grew weary of its weight, and when he reached the upper world, he decided to peep into the sack before he took a rest. He cut a small hole, and the stars came flying out to fill the heavens. Only a few remained when he shut the sack, afraid of Ut'set's anger. She cursed him with blindness, then took the remaining stars and placed them in the heavens to form the Great Bear, Orion and the Pleiades.

— Zia

More than any other group of native myths, those relating to the stars and constellations are strikingly uniform across the continent. Most frequently mentioned are the Great Bear, Orion and the Pleiades, often attributed to a chase in which the pursued flees into the sky followed by pursuers who are eternally frustrated. This is a natural description of the "feet" of Ursa Major and its three hunters. Apt and poetic descriptions of the Pleiades as a group of dancers, or of the Corona Borealis as a council circle, are also widespread. Venus (as the morning star) and the Pole Star are the individual stars mentioned most frequently. The Morning Star is generally thought of as a warrior, sometimes as the messenger of the sun, sometimes as a maiden. The Pawnee, among whom star myths are especially abundant and vivid, think of the Polar Star as the chief of the night skies. The Milky Way is widely regarded as the Great Spirit Path.

Many legends surround the Pleiades, described as either sisters or brothers trapped in the sky, usually engaged in an eternal dance:

The Pleiades were a group of brothers who were awakened in the night by singing voices to which they began to dance. As they danced, the voices receded and they followed them, drawn little by little into the sky where the pitying moon transformed them into a group of fixed stars and bade them to dance for ten days each year over the council house of the Red Men, during the season of their New Year. One of the dancing brothers, however, hearing the weeping of his mother, looked backward and fell with such force that he was buried in the earth. The mother mourned for a year over his grave from which appeared a tiny sprout which grew into a tree that aspired to the heavens, and so was born the Pine, the tallest of trees, the guide of the forest, and the watcher of the skies.

— Traditional

The Plains peoples incorporated their lifeways, including the buffalo hunt, into their legends of the night sky, as in the story of the Pleiades as the Lost Children:

There is a family of six stars we call the Lost Children. One spring day, when the buffalo calves were yellow, the hunters killed many animals and gave the small yellow hides to the children to wear as they played buffalo. A poor family of six children were unable to secure any of the skins, and so they went naked. The other children taunted them as they played, and the six children wandered away on the plains and were taken up to the sky. When the buffalo calves are yellow [in spring], the Lost Children cannot be seen, but when the calves turn brown [in the fall], the Lost Children are visible in the sky.

— Blackfoot legend

he weather was often perceived as an eternal conflict between the powers of the Earth or the underworld and those of the skies, symbolized by the legendary Thunderbird. Thunder was its province and that of its helpers, especially the eagles and hawks, of which Keneu, the Golden Eagle, was among the most important. The Thunderbird was sometimes described as an enormous bird that bore a lake on its back. Its eyes flashed bolts of lightning, and the beating of its wings produced claps of thunder. Opposing evil spirits that parched the earth and withered the grasses, the Thunderers brought rain. They were often seen in visions and were perceived as tutelary spirits, especially on the Great Plains. There, thunderstorms were often thought of as conflicts between the Thunderbird and a fearsome monster of the underworld that the Sioux called Unktehi. The Plains peoples believed that the Thunderbird announced the coming of the regeneration of life in the spring with great claps of thunder, and in the Great Lakes region, its huge wings were believed to create the winds, while its eyes flashed lightning.

Among the Iroquois, the thunder god Hino was attended by the analogous Dew Eagle—another aspect of the Thunderbird spirit. The Dew Eagle Oshadagea lived in the western sky and carried a lake of dew in the hollow of its back. When the evil spirits of fire burned the green grasses, Oshadagea brought healing dew on his outspread wings. The Zuñi believed that thunder was caused when Rain-makers rolled gaming stones in the heavens, and that flashes of lightning were the trajectories of arrows shot by celestial archers.

We should be as water, which is lower than all things yet stronger even than the rocks.

—OGLALA SIOUX PROVERB

These pages: *Traditional Northwest Coast images of "the winged peoples" included such supernatural powers as the mighty Thunderbird and the legendary Keneu, the Golden Eagle, both monarchs of the sky who brought thunder, lightning and life-giving rain.*

The Great Thunderbird

The great thunderbird, Wakinyan Tanka, once built his tipi on Paha Sapa. But when the white man came to this sacred mountain, the Wakinyan fled to where the sun goes down—a pristine dwelling guarded by a butterfly, a bear, a deer and a beaver.

Swathed in clouds, the thunderbirds come from the four points of the compass, their wings spread wide and armed with claws and sharp teeth. Their voices are loud claps of thunder; low rumblings are the echoes of their children. Inside the Great Wakinyan's tipi, thunderbirds are hatched from a giant egg upon a warm nest of dry bones.

Invisible in robes of grey clouds, the Wakinyan test your courage in a dream quest, and though their rolling thunder and their zig-zag lightning may frighten, they are helping spirits and guardians of the truth. The thunderbirds bring rain and fire and help to mankind. But beware of swearing falsely on the sacred pipe, for then the Wakinyan will kill with bolts of lightning. Once in a great while a holy man may catch a glimpse of a Wakinyan in a dream—but only a glimpse.

The Unktehi or water monster, on the other hand, hated humans from the beginning of creation. Her scaly body filled the great Missouri River, while smaller water monsters took over lakes and streams.

"Who are these vile creatures creeping on the earth?" the water monsters asked each other. "Let's get rid of them."

Puffing up her body, the Great Unktehi caused the Missouri River to overflow its banks; her children swamped the lakes and streams, flooding the land and killing the people. The few who survived sought safety on the highest mountains.

"We must save these helpless people from the Unktehi," the great thunderbird declared, unleashing a battle against the evil water monsters. Flashes of lightning turned night into day, the earth quaked and the waters flowed in torrents. Though the Wakinyan fought with all their might, the Unktehi were winning.

"Our power is in the heavens," the Great Wakinyan said, taking council with the thunder beings on their sacred mountain. "It was a mistake for us to fight the Unktehi on the earth. Let us hurl our thunderbolts and sheets of lightning instead."

The earth burned fiery red, the waters dried up and all the Unktehi perished in the Badlands where their bones turned into stone. And the Wakinyan gained power over the waters. The humans who found safety on the high rock gave praise to the Wakinyan and again they peopled the earth. All this happened in the age of Tunka, the Rock.

—SIOUX LEGEND

Mother Earth

We are made from Mother Earth and we shall all go back to Mother Earth.

—SHENANDOAH BELIEF

Opposite: *Collecting water in a desert oasis:* Mother Earth Providing a Garden of Eden, *photographed by Edward S. Curtis.*

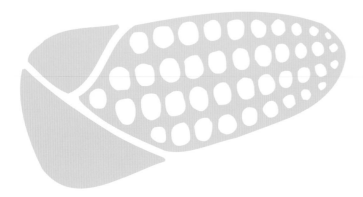

The earth is the mother of all people, and all people should have equal rights upon it.

—CHIEF JOSEPH, NEZ PERCÉ

The personification of the Earth as the mother of life and the giver of food is virtually universal in indigenous cultures throughout the world, and certainly prevailed among the native peoples of North America.

The earth was placed here for us…and we consider her our Mother. How much would you ask for if your Mother had been harmed? No amount of money can repay. Money cannot give birth to anything.

—ASA BAZHONOODAH, NAVAJO

Algonquian peoples address Mother Earth as Nokomis, or "Grandmother," and the Iroquois as Eithinoha, "Our Mother," of whom they say:

The earth is living matter, and the tender plantlet of the bean and the sprouting germ of corn nestling therein receive through their delicate rootlets the life substance from the Earth….Earth feeds itself to them; since what is supplied to them is living matter, life in them is produced and conserved, and as food the ripened corn and bean and their kinds, thus produced, create and develop the life of man and of all living things.

—IROQUOIS TRADITION

Although held in universal awe, Mother Earth was not seen as an omnipotent, jealous goddess who demanded sacrifices; rather, she was seen as nurturer and protector of all life.

You ask me to plow the ground. Shall I take a knife and tear my mother's bosom? Then when I die she will not take me to her bosom to rest.

You ask me to dig for stones! Shall I dig under her skin for her bones? Then when I die I cannot enter her body to be reborn again.

You ask me to cut grass and make hay and sell it, and be rich like white men, but how dare I cut my mother's hair?

I want my people to stay with me here. All the dead men will come to life again. Their spirits will come to their bodies again. We must wait here in the homes of our fathers and be ready to meet them in the bosom of our mother.

—WOVOKA, PAIUTE

Take only what you need and leave the land as you found it.

—ARAPAHO PROVERB

The Lakota was a true naturalist—a lover of Nature. He loved the earth and all things of the earth, and the attachment grew with age. The old people came literally to love the soil and they sat or reclined on the ground with a feeling of being close to a mothering power. It was good for the skin to touch the earth, and the old people liked to remove their moccasins and walk with bare feet on the sacred earth. Their tipis were built upon the earth and their altars were made of earth. The birds that flew in the air came to rest upon the earth, and it was the final abiding place of all things that lived and grew. The soil was soothing, strengthening, cleansing and healing.

—LUTHER STANDING BEAR, TETON SIOUX

Native Americans across the continent learn traditional skills passed down through the generations in the cultivation, lore and uses of plant life. Many believed that every animal-borne disease could be cured by an herbal antidote. The significance of maize was celebrated in annual ceremonies, including the Green Corn or Busk ritual: The corn was infused with a powerful spirit of renewal as the sacred fire was rekindled and the spirit of community affirmed in joyful celebration. Spirits of maize and other cultivated plants are common in the mythologies of all agricultural peoples. They are usually feminine in nature (although the Algonquian Mondamin is an important exception). Corn, Squash and Beans form a maiden triad in Iroquois myth. In the Southwest, a myriad of corn spirits are celebrated. Hopi girls of marriageable age traditionally wear their hair in two whorls at the sides of the head, imitating the squash blossom, a symbol of fertility.

If the balance of nature were not respected, if humans took too much from the earth or violated it in any way,

these powers could strike back. Thus Native Americans were shocked at the European's brutal exploitation of the earth and its creatures:

The white people never cared for the land or deer or bear. When we Indians kill meat, we eat it all up. When we dig roots, we make little holes. When we build houses, we make little holes. When we burn grass for grasshoppers, we don't ruin things. We shake down acorns and pinenuts. We don't chop down the trees. We only use dead wood. But the white people plow up the ground, pull down the trees, kill everything. The tree says, "Don't. I am sore. Don't hurt me." But they chop it down and cut it up. The spirit of the land hates them. They blast out trees and stir it up to its depths. They saw up the trees. That hurts them. The Indians never hurt anything, but the white people destroy all. They blast rocks and scatter them on the ground. The rock says, "Don't! You are hurting me." But the white people pay no attention. When the Indians use rocks, they take the little round ones for their cooking....How can the spirit of the earth like the white man?...Everywhere the white man has touched it, it is sore.

—WINTU ELDER

Opposite: "Praying to the Spirits at Crater Lake," *a Curtis portrait of a Klamath in his pristine environment.*

*To touch the Earth is to
be in harmony with nature.*
—NORTHERN PLAINS PROVERB

Amulets, Charms and Sacred Objects

The outline of the stone is round, having no end and no beginning; like the power of the stone it is endless.

—CHASED-BY-BEARS, SANTEE-YANKTONAI SIOUX

Natural objects could be infused with spiritual power by being struck with lightning, exposed to the smoke of the sacred fire or of ritual tobacco, immersed in swiftly running water, or in other ways. Holy people possessed sacred stones, quartz crystals and other powerful objects that were highly prized. Valuable "sacred bundles" of such objects were traded, and many tribes guarded them from generation to generation. The Cherokee kept such revered objects in a special palanquin. Several Lower Mississippi tribes housed idols, sacred icons and sacred objects in their temples and ceremonial buildings.

Supernatural power was taken seriously, and sacred objects that carried it could be dangerous. Their use entailed purification and ritual, to prevent profanation and consequent misuse or loss of power. Shamans and medicine men or women guarded the rules and rituals governing their use. The Creek "war bundle" was carried on the back of the war ceremonialist and was never allowed to touch the ground. During the Omaha buffalo hunt, a woman was appointed to keep the sacred white buffalo hide, which was carefully guarded in a tipi by night. If this were not done, the hunt would fail.

Ritual incantations or spells were often the closely guarded secrets of the shaman, medicine man, or tribal elder. Their creation was usually attributed to a revered ancestor with special power. Such secrets could be used for many purposes: to cure illness, to bring good weather and abundant harvests, to ensure victory in war, to win love.

Stones were prominent among sacred objects. They evoked the power of the living earth that had thrust them to the surface from great depths. The flint that gave off sparks when struck, and the rocks that shaped the tools were venerated.

A traditional Omaha sweat-lodge ceremony involves an invocation to the seven spirits (those of the four cardinal directions, and those above, below and at the center). The sacred healing stones are placed in the middle of the group to represent the center:

O! Aged One,
At a time when there were gathered together seven persons,
You sat in the seventh place, it is said,
And of the Seven you alone possessed knowledge of all things.
When in their longing for protection and guidance,
The people sought in their minds for a way,
They beheld you seated with assured permanency and
*   endurance,*
In the center where converged the paths,
There, exposed to the violence of the four winds, you sat,
Possessed with power to receive supplications,
O! Aged One.

—OMAHA PRAYER

The Magic of the Stones

All the young braves wanted to marry Yaada, the loveliest daughter of the Haida tribe. But an old, old medicine man who was powerful and rich declared, "Yaada shall be my wife."

And a handsome fisherman who was gloriously young, and at the same time desperately poor, also proclaimed, "Yaada shall be my wife."

"Why not give my daughter to the great medicine man, for he has awesome power and vast riches," Yaada's mother dreamed. Yet, her heart melting like wax in summer sunshine, she wavered: "Ulka has a boy's heart and he is brave and strong. Why not give her to him?"

But the laws of the great Haida tribe decreed, "Give the girl to the greatest man. The man of magic must have his way."

Then Yaada herself spoke: "It is not riches nor beauty that make a good husband. Let us test the excellence of these two men, for only then can I choose who is to be the father of my children. Let each one throw a stone so we can see the evil or the beauty of their hearts. I shall marry the one who makes the noblest mark."

"Alas!" lamented the Haida mother, "This casting of stones proves prowess, not worth."

"The spirit of my father will help me judge," the girl replied, "So they must cast stones."

Never did the medicine man look so old, so wrinkled, so palsied, nor Ulka so young, so brave, so beautiful. The girl loved the young man dearly, but she was bound by the spirit of her ancestors.

With greed in his heart and in his thoughts, the great medicine man chanted his magic as his withered fingers flung the first stone. Like lightning, it shattered a great rock, opening the "Grey Archway" that has remained to this day.

"O wondrous magic," the tribe exclaimed, awed that even the rocks did his bidding.

Yaada stood by in anguish, Ulka at her side. Just as the young man took a smooth, flat stone, the medicine man pinned his poisonous eyes upon him and uttered an evil incantation. As the stone left his strong fingers it curved and struck the forehead of Yaada's mother, and she fell into the final sleep.

"Slayer of my mother!" the girl raged at the medicine man. "Your black magic reveals your black heart. You cared not for my sorrow."

"The medicine man poisons the very air we breathe," the tribe exclaimed, for they had witnessed the evil deed. "His heart is black and cold as night. But the young man is blameless as the sun."

Yaada raised her voice in a sorrowful chant:

My feet shall walk no more upon this island,
With its great, Grey Archway.
My mother sleeps forever on this island,
With its great, Grey Archway.
My heart would break without her on this island,
With its great, Grey Archway.

In her grief Yaada moved to the edge of a cliff. "Ulka, you are innocent. It was your rival who slew my mother," she cried to her beloved. "I must go to her. Will you stay or come with me?"

The slender youth sprang to her side and took her hand in his, and they paused on the brink of the rocks. With the radiance of stars, they plunged together into the sea.

Yaada and Ulka can still be seen today: They are two silvery fish leaping and diving together near the great, Grey Archway where they first set out to find the soul of Yadda's mother.

—HAIDA LEGEND

The Power and Spirits of Animals

The frog does not drink up the pond in which he lives.

—SIOUX PROVERB

What is life? It is the flash of a firefly in the night. It is the breath of a buffalo in the winter time. It is the little shadow which runs across the grass and loses itself in the Sunset.

—CROWFOOT, BLACKFOOT

The hunting peoples of North America—and even those who depended mainly on agriculture—revered the spirits of animals, who were seen as strong, swift and splendidly adapted to the natural world. This respect is seen in the words of Teton Sioux chief Luther Standing Bear:

For the Lakota, mountains, lakes, rivers, springs, valleys and woods were all finished beauty. Winds, rain, snow, sunshine, day, night and change of seasons were endlessly fascinating. Birds, insects and animals filled the world with knowledge that defied the comprehension of man.

—LUTHER STANDING BEAR, TETON SIOUX

It was widely believed that animals had souls, and some legends told that animals could assume human form at will. Many believed that animals were immortal creatures who willingly surrendered their bodies to the hunter, while their spirits left to be born anew. Others learned that animals had inhabited the world before humanity—that they might well have participated in creation. One such story tells that:

Great Hare was on a raft in the midst of the waters with the other animals. Nothing could be seen except for the waterfowl. The Beaver dived, seeking a grain of soil; for the Great Hare had assured the animals that with even one grain he could create land. Nevertheless, the Beaver returned unsuccessful. Then the Muskrat tried, and he was gone nearly an entire day. When he reappeared, apparently dead, his four feet were tightly clenched; but in one of them was a single grain of sand, and from this the earth was made and it grew into the form of a mountain surrounded by water, the height ever increasing, even to this day, as the Great Hare courses around it.

—MONTAGNAIS MYTH

When people came into the world, many legends tell, the animals retreated into the forests and to their own villages and settlements, where they assumed human form. Favored humans could learn the wisdom of the animal spirits if they observed them patiently.

The Dakota understood the meaning of self-sacrifice, perhaps because their legends taught them that the buffalo, on which their very life depended, gave itself voluntarily that they might live.

—ELLA DELORIA, DAKOTA SIOUX

Below: *The sacred buffalo.*

All hunters sought a communion with animals. They needed to learn their ways and show respect to them if they were to succeed in the hunt. Countless rituals governed the relationship of humans to animals, especially those related to food and its preparation.

Hunting was governed by a complex array of religious attitudes, rituals and taboos. The slaying of a beast was a moment of deeply felt realization, a kind of apotheosis. Hunters approached their quarry reverently, taking only what they needed and avoiding the infliction of unnecessary pain. Even the bones of a kill were revered and respected; they had to be protected from dogs and other beasts.

> *What is man without the beasts? If all the beasts were gone, men would die from great loneliness of spirit, for whatever happens to the beasts also happens to man. All things are connected. Whatever befalls the earth befalls the children of the earth.*
>
> —CHIEF SEATHL

If a hunter did not observe the rituals and taboos, if he was cruel, disrespectful, or overhunted or overfished, the animals would simply withdraw and disappear, and the hunter would find no game. Luther Standing Bear stated that:

> *Kinship with all creatures of the earth, sky, and water [is] a real and active principle....The animals had rights — the right to man's protection, the right to live, the right to multiply, the right to freedom, and the right to man's indebtedness — and in recognition of these rights the Lakota never enslaved an animal, and spared all life that was not needed for food and clothing.*
>
> —LUTHER STANDING BEAR, TETON SIOUX

Before eating, always take a little time to thank the food
—ARAPAHO PROVERB

Humans could acquire animal powers through the magic of appropriation. Wearing a deerskin gave one the power to run like a deer; wearing the tail of a fox conferred the cunning of the fox; the feathers of an eagle, nobility and freedom; the claws of a bear, strength and courage. The hawk's wing was associated with speed; the claw of a squirrel with skill in climbing. The skin of a seabird or a seal would bring success in fishing.

Opposite: Hunting for salmon in a Northwestern river with spears, a skill requiring speed and silent agility.

Below: A Cree moose hunter sounding a horn to lure his prey.

Everything was possessed of personality, only differing from us in form. Knowledge was inherent in all things. The world was a library and its books were the stones, leaves, grass, brooks and the birds and animals that shared, alike with us, the storms and blessings of earth. We learned to do what only the student of nature ever learns, and that was to feel beauty. We never railed at the storms, the furious winds, and the biting frosts and snows.

Even the lightning did us no harm, for whenever it came too close, mothers and grandmothers in every tipi put cedar leaves on the coals and their magic kept danger away. Bright days and dark days were both expressions of the Great Mystery.

—LUTHER STANDING BEAR, TETON SIOUX

They shall offer thanks to the earth where all people dwell—

To the streams of water, the pools, the springs and the lakes; to the maize and the fruits—

To the medicinal herbs and the trees, to the forest trees for their usefulness, to the animals that serve as food and who offer their pelts as clothing—

To the great winds and the lesser winds; to the Thunderers; and the Sun, the mighty warrior; to the moon—

To the messengers of the Great Spirit who dwells in the skies above, who gives all things useful to men, who is the source and the ruler of health and life.

—IROQUOIS CONSTITUTION

Dreams and Visions

You ask me to plow the ground. Shall I take a knife and tear my mother's bosom? Then when I die she will not take me to her bosom to rest.

You ask me to dig for stones! Shall I dig under her skin for her bones? Then when I die I cannot enter her body to be reborn again.

You ask me to cut grass and make hay and sell it, and be rich like white men, but how dare I cut my mother's hair?

I want my people to stay with me here. All the dead men will come to life again. Their spirits will come to their bodies again. We must wait here in the homes of our fathers and be ready to meet them in the bosom of our mother.

—WOVOKA, PAIUTE

Dreams are wiser than men.

— OMAHA

reams are a way of communing with one's own spirit, of drawing out the gifts and needs of that spirit for inspiration in responding to life's many choices and challenges. Dreaming opens the door to new ways of fostering well-being in oneself and others. In many Native American cultures, dreams can explain the causes of sickness and reveal methods of curing it. Across the continent, children have long been encouraged to pay close attention to their dreams and learn to understand their messages.

Some North American peoples believed that individuals possess a dream soul — a spirit free to leave the sleeping body and travel to distant lands, or other psychic realms. Shamans often had to seek a patient's dream soul to restore him or her to health. The dream soul could seek a wider view of events on earth, or prophesy the future. Countless stories recount the prophetic dreams of elders who foresaw the coming of the Europeans, like this vision of an Ojibwa prophet:

I dreamed that men of strange appearance have come across the great water and landed on our island. Their skins are white like snow, and hair grows on their faces. These people have come across the great water in large canoes with wings like those of a giant white bird. The men have long, sharp knives and black tubes that they point at birds and animals. The tubes make smoke like the smoke from our pipes, and they make deafening noises that were terrifying even in my dream.

— OJIBWA

Opposite: "Placating the Spirit of a Slain Eagle," a *Curtis portrait of an Assiniboine warrior.*

Pay heed to the voices in your dreams.

—CHEYENNE PROVERB

The peoples of the Northeast accorded great importance to dreams. They valued them as guides to cultivating good fortune in many areas of life, and were especially aware of their power to show the causes and treatments of illness. Gifted persons could acquire the power to cure through visions and dreams. They were a means of deepening self-understanding of one's talent or vocation, whether for warfare, hunting, healing, or various crafts.

Across the Great Plains, visions received by elders and other holy people in dreams have great influence, especially as prophecy and instruction. In another prophetic

dream of the coming of the Europeans, a Cheyenne wise man cautioned his people:

Some day you will meet a people who are white. They will try always to give you things, but do not take them. If you take these things they offer you, they will bring you sickness.

—SWEET MEDICINE, CHEYENNE

Dreams of great significance were not only experienced by tribal elders, but could also occur in childhood. Some were powerful enough to remain vivid in the dreamer's memory across a lifetime and exert a guiding influence through their messages:

When I was ten years of age I looked at the land and the rivers, the sky above, and the animals around me and could not fail to realize that they were made by some great power. I was so anxious to understand this power that I questioned the trees and the bushes. It seemed as though the flowers were staring at me, and I wanted to ask them "Who made you?" I looked at the moss-covered stones; some of them seemed to have the features of a man, but they could not answer me. Then I had a dream, and in my dream one of these small round stones appeared to me and told me that the maker of all was Wakan tanka, and that in order to honor him, I must honor his works in nature. The stone said that by my search I had shown myself worthy of supernatural help. It said that if I were curing a sick person, I might ask its assistance, and that all the forces of nature would help me work a cure.

—BRAVE BUFFALO, SIOUX

Right: A Blackfoot travois, photographed by Edward Curtis.

The Lazy Boy's Dream

Once there lived a young boy, the son of rich parents, who became lazy and spoiled. The boy expected everything to be done for him. His mother, sad and frustrated by his growing indolence, decided he must learn to participate in the work of his people, so, one day, she asked him to help prepare the food for the coming winter.

The boy's task was to tend the fish as it was cooking and remove the bad foam from the top of the boiling fish pot. Sulking, the boy found the work tedious, and soon became cross. In his temper, he threw some of the hot water from the pot at a little mouse, scalding it badly.

When winter came, the men of the tribe went out in search of game, as usual. But this year, there were no animals to be seen. There was only the last of the summer fish to eat; by midwinter, the snows were deeper and the winds colder than ever, and the preserved fish ran out. Everyone was hungry, and still no game could be found.

One cold night, the young boy could not tolerate his hunger pangs any longer: He ventured out in search of something to eat. But he felt weak, and eventually he sat down and fell asleep. Then, he heard the voice of a woman, and when he looked up he saw a warm fire burning inside a house. An old woman was sitting on a chair beside the fire, beckoning him to enter.

"Young man," she said as he walked in, "you have done something wrong and you have caused the famine that has befallen your people. Have you harmed an animal?"

Trembling, the boy confessed that he had scalded a little mouse when he had been in a bad mood. Then he saw that the poor scarred mouse was sitting by the woman's chair. He was filled with remorse at his own cruelty, and knelt down to apologize to the woman and to the mouse. "Please forgive me," he begged, "and do not punish my people for my wrongdoing. I am truly sorry for the pain I have caused."

The woman recognized that the boy's sorrow was genuine. She invited him to dine with her and then told him that the famine would end.

When the boy awoke, he understood that his dream carried a lesson. He had grown up and learned lessons of personal responsibility and respect for living creatures—lessons that he needed to become a man. As he headed for home, he heard the sounds of caribou; he slew one of the animals and carried the food home for his people. The boy's mother was overjoyed, because she saw that the lazy boy had matured and grown and had gone out to hunt for food like a responsible young man.

—NORTHERN ATHAPASCAN LEGEND

Wisdom comes to us in dreams.

— WOVOKA, PAIUTE

Perhaps the best-known visionary of the Plains and Plateau regions was Wovoka, a Paiute who acquired his spiritual powers through his father. During a solar eclipse, Wovoka had a vision of the Ghost Dance revival of 1889. He soon became an influential leader and prophet, mobilizing his people and several neighboring Plains tribes to resist the destructive incursions of westward migration and soldiers sent to protect the settlers. In his vision, Wovoka dreamed of a better world, faithful to the ways of the ancestors, that could be resurrected through the ritual Ghost Dance.

When I was in the other world with the Old Man, I saw all the people who have died. But they were not sad. They were in a pleasant land, green and rich with an abundance of game and fish, and everyone was eternally young. After showing me all of heaven, the Old Man told me to go back to earth and tell His people to be good and love one another and to live in peace. Then He gave me this dance to give to my people.

— WOVOKA, PAIUTE

Left: *Brule Sioux leader Short Bull, an influential member of the Ghost Dance movement.*

Opposite: *The totem pole, an emblem of clan kinship between the human and animal worlds.*

The Pole that Holds Up the Sky

Long ago, there lived a chief named Wakiash, who was sad because he had never had a totem pole, and without a totem pole he could not host a dance. He was also ashamed, because chiefs were expected to hold great dances for the people. One day, Wakiash went up into the mountains and fasted to seek guidance. After four days, he fell into a deep sleep. A frog fell on him, and Wakiash awoke. "Come!" exclaimed the frog. "We will fly around the world on Raven's back."

Raven carried the chief and the frog all over the land. After four days, they flew over a house with a fine totem pole; they could hear the sounds of laughter and singing from within the house. Raven stopped and set them down outside the door. "Quick," said the frog, "hide with me, then jump into the house when the dancing begins."

Inside the house were many animals, but they did not begin their dance because they could feel the presence of intruders. A mouse was sent outside to see who was there. The little mouse soon found Wakiash and the frog, butWakiash persuaded the mouse not to chase them away; he gave him a piece of goat's fat as a friendly gesture. The mouse thanked him and asked, "Why did you come here?"

"I want to learn to dance and to have a fine totem pole," the chief replied. So the mouse led Wakiash and the frog into the house, promising to teach the chief what he needed to learn. Wakiash patiently watched and listened to the teachings of the animals, and copied their movements as they danced their different steps. Eventually, the masked animal chief told Wakiash that he was ready to return home with his new-found knowledge, and that he should take with him a medicine bundle.

Raven carried Wakiash, the frog and the medicine bundle back to the mountains. Wakiash awoke from his deep sleep and took the medicine bundle back home. The next morning, the medicine bundle was gone, but in its place was a magnificent totem pole with all the animals that had been painted on Wakiash's house: the whale, bear, raven and smaller animals. To celebrate this joyous happening, Wakiash held a dance—the best dance anyone could remember.

The day after the dance, the totem pole disappeared, but Wakiash now knew what he needed to build a new one. He concentrated on everything he had learned from the animals in his dream, realizing that the frog had shown him the importance of honoring the animals that had protected his own ancestors. Wakiash fashioned a tall new totem pole that was more majestic even than the last one. He called it Kulakuyuwish— the pole that holds up the sky.

—KWAKIUTL LEGEND

All their wisdom and knowledge came to them in dreams. They tested their dreams, and in that way learned their own strength.

— OJIBWA

Among the native peoples of the Colorado River basin in California, dreams were the most important window into the supernatural world. The migratory Yuma believed that the universe was animated by a single all-pervasive force that could be contacted only through dreams. Thus, one could acquire the kind of personal power deemed essential to personal growth, fulfillment, or success in any activity. Sequences of tribal mythology and history were acquired or recovered in dreams, then converted into songs and acted out in ceremonies. The Yuma were especially aware of the power that a religious or military leader could acquire in this way. It took priority over all other activities—farming, food-gathering, hunting. Each village had a shaman, or "keeper of the smoke," who presided over the ceremonial life inspired by dreams.

The Pima Papago villagers of the Southwest also valued the supernatural powers connected with dreams, singing, visions and intoxication. They balanced this with attention to the demands imposed by the harsh conditions of their environment: drought and flood that often threatened their farming, hunting and food-gathering for the community.

Opposite: *Spider Rock, in Arizona's Canyon de Chelly National Monument, is a landmark revered by the Navajo.*

Above: *The dream catcher, a well-known ritual artefact among the Southwestern peoples for harnessing the power of dreams.*

Vision Quest

To go on a vision quest is to go into the presence of the great mystery.

—LAKOTA PROVERB

The vision quest is almost always an individual act undertaken on behalf of the community. Traditionally, it was supported most strongly by the medicine men and tribal elders, who would help prepare a young man (or, less frequently, a young woman) to set out in search of communion with supernatural powers and the acquisition of a guardian spirit through the visionary experience. Visions were generally sought in solitary places—deep in the woods, or on a hill or mountain top—that were associated with the spirit power of whom the vision was sought. The supplicant prepared for the quest with purifying sweat baths, pipe rituals, prayer, meditation and fasting. The solitary vigil could last up to seven nights and days. The spirit power generally appeared in the form of a man, woman, animal, or bird; sometimes these apparitions of guardian spirits transformed from animal to human shape, or assumed other natural forms.

If a vision and communion with the guardian spirit were achieved, the spirit would confer the kind of supernatural power best suited to the quester's needs and mission in life. The guardian spirit also taught the youth how to use and cherish these supernatural gifts. An Iroquois legend recounts such a rite of passage:

A thousand years ago, a boy went forth to become a man. He entered the woods alone, without provisions of any kind, and built himself a modest shelter of branches and bark and lit a small fire outside. He then lay down to fast and dream for three days and nights, hoping to entertain a spiritual visitor—a manitou—a guide who would teach him his future and life work.

The boy was lucky: A great Manitou appeared to him on the first night. Into the glow of the boy's small fire stepped a beautiful and strong young man, decked all in green and yellow. The young man signaled to the boy to come wrestle with him. All night the boy wrestled with the Manitou, like Jacob with the Angel. At dawn, the young man disappeared. He returned the next night and they wrestled again.

On the third night the young man spoke. He told the boy to overcome him, and to kill and bury him on the spot. The boy was then to return throughout the summer to pour water on the grave and tend it. In the fall, the Great Spirit's gift to the people would appear.

Grieving but obedient, the boy killed and buried the beautiful young man and tended his grave. A green shoot sprang from the ground and grew tall. It bore green-wrapped ears of maize, the gift of the Great Spirit to the people.

—IROQUOIS LEGEND

Opposite: *The powerful Curtis photograph* The Eagle Catcher *embodies the spirit of the vision quest.*

*Knowledge is of
the past; wisdom is
of the future.*
—VERNON COOPER, LUMBEE

If we wonder often, the gift of knowledge will come.

—ARAPAHO PROVERB

In a vision quest, the supplicant might be taught medicine for hunting, for healing, for war, or for the role of a shaman or medicine man. The guardian spirit would instruct him or her on the meaning and value of the objects to be included in the sacred medicine bundle. Sometimes the spirit imparted sacred chants and songs by which it could be recalled at need.

For the peoples of the Great Plains and the Plateau, visionary communion with the spirit world was crucial to success in life, and the spirit quest was among the most important rituals—the gateway to the status and responsibilities of adulthood. In some tribes, young women entered adulthood through a spirit quest at the time of their first menses. The testimony of those who have experienced powerful visions speaks to their importance for personal growth.

Above: A traditional peace pipe used in preparation for a vision quest and other ceremonial rites.

Left: Mandan Chief Four Bears, in an 1832 portrait by George Catlin.

Opposite, top: Makah, an elder Blackfoot woman of the Motokiks sacred female society.

Opposite, bottom: A desert spring sacred to the Zuñi, as depicted in a nineteenth-century engraving.

I fasted for four years, and the spirits above, even as far as the fourth heaven, all approved of my going. They blessed me. Ten days I fasted and after that I fasted twenty days; and again I fasted thirty days. All the spirits blessed me, even those under the earth.

Then when I was ready to go to the earth, all the spirits gathered around me and had a council. In the center of the world, there, they had a council. There they were to advise me. All the spirits were present. They told me that I would not fail in anything I attempted. There they tested my powers.

The lodge was full of spirits. Then they started to sing the songs that I was to use when on earth. After that, I walked around the fireplace, and taking a live coal, I held it in the palm of my hand and danced around the fireplace again. Then I shouted "wahi!" and struck the hand containing the live coal with the other hand.

—THUNDERCLOUD, WINNEBAGO

Below: A Sun Dancer has bound himself to a lodgepole by thongs threaded into his chest: For Strength and Visions, *a memorable portrait by Curtis.*

Visionary experiences were not only sought in solitude, but sometimes communally in a ritual or ceremonial. One such ritual was the Sun Dance, which developed in different forms throughout the Great Plains culture area. Usually performed at or near the summer solstice, participants gathered at a ceremonial lodge or sacred place and performed dances, drumming, songs and meditation over several days, fasting throughout. Male dancers sometimes pierced their skin over the breastbone and threaded thongs that tied them to a central lodgepole, then danced until their flesh was ripped. Through their self-mortification and pain, they sought visions and blessings.

While the pledger of the ceremony was dancing up and down with his gaze riveted on the holy image in the rear of the lodge, a dozen young men were undergoing torture for their own ends. Some were dragging through camp two buffalo skulls fastened to a stick thrust through holes cut in their backs. Others —and Takes-the-pipe among them —decided to swing from the lodge poles. So he begged Sharp-horn to pierce the flesh above his breasts, run skewers through the openings, and tie the rods to ropes hung from a pole. Thus attached he ran back and forth till he had torn out the skewers. Yet when he had fallen to the ground faint and blood-stained no vision came for all his pains.

He wanted to become a chief like Shinbone, so he went on a mountain peak to fast....He slept there overnight.... Suddenly he heard a man clearing his throat and a horse's neighing came closer and closer. A voice behind him said, "The one whom you wanted to come has arrived."

—CROW

Opposite: Ritual masks, totem poles, carved dugouts and other imposing artefacts make the Northwestern culture area one of complex, vivid symbols.

We do face the sun and pray to God through the sun, asking for strength to complete the Sun Dance, and that our prayers will be heard…and in the sun we see visions.

—FRANK FOOLS CROW, LAKOTA SIOUX

Some tribes believed that the powers obtained in visionary experiences could be transferred to others who had not been blessed with such apparitions. The Northwestern peoples also believed that individuals could enhance their personal power through contact and communion with the spirit world in prayer and visions. The Salish tribes accorded special importance to this, believing that success in any domain resulted from the gifts bestowed through such contacts. Unlike groups in other regions, young Salish men were not encouraged to seek visions at puberty. Their emphasis was on the hereditary transmission of spirit contacts experienced by an ancestor. These spirit contacts were represented symbolically by totemic objects called "crests," which were handed down in the potlatch ceremony.

Shamans and Medicine People

The purpose of medicine is power.

—AGNES WHISTLING ELK, CREE

 hamans—ecstatic visionaries and healers—play a vital role in Native American life. Early explorers and missionaries applied the term "medicine man" to those who healed the sick. However, the best English equivalent for the term "medicine" in native languages is "supernatural power." Through privileged contact with one or more tutelary spirits, shamans—usually men— acquire a broad range of supernatural powers and instruction in the rituals governing their use. Their learning continues throughout their lifetimes, and their powers evolve and grow with their increasing experience and wisdom. With these powers, shamans cure disease; control such natural phenomena as the weather; divine the future; locate enemies, game and lost objects; and expose dishonesty and malign influences. As religious leaders, they conduct rituals conducive to community well-being. As representatives of beneficent powers, they protect the tribe from the forces of evil, sometimes including evil shamans. They are usually exceptional people: sensitive, intuitive, meditative, visionary, or volatile. Respected, often feared, their clans or tribes offer them material support.

A Blackfoot shaman named Smoking-Star told the story of how he began to acquire his powers:

By the third day [of my vision quest] I was too exhausted to stand. That night I lay on my back looking up at the sky. Then I saw the Smoking-Star. And as I gazed, it came nearer and nearer. Then I heard a voice: "My son, why do you cry here?" Then I saw a fine warrior on the ground before me, smoking my pipe. At last he said, "I will give you power. You are to take my name. You must never change it. Always pray to me and I will help you."

In the course of time, everyone came to look upon me as a shaman. No one will now walk before me as I sit in a tipi. In my presence, all are dignified and orderly and avoid frivolous talk. Four times in my life the Smoking-Star has stood before me.

—SMOKING-STAR, BLACKFOOT

Opposite: *The buffalo robe clothed its wearer in the power of this sacred animal.*

The first peace is that which comes within the souls of men when they realize their relationship, their oneness, with the universe and all its powers.

—BLACK ELK, OGLALA LAKOTA

Opposite: Petroglyphs depicting shamanic spirit figures in the Barrier Canyon style at Utah's Sego Canyon.

In a world permeated with spiritual forces the shaman's experience is a special form of that power which is available in various degrees to everyone. Many men and women received supernatural power and the conditions governing its use, whether for hunting, leadership, healing, or warfare, but few became shamans. In some tribes the role was hereditary, but even so, the person's power was usually confirmed and manifested through spiritual intervention.

Violent illness or emotional disturbance were sometimes regarded as signs that an individual was favored by the spirit world but resistant to his or her role as a shaman, which carried both great responsibility and dangers unknown to ordinary mortals. Such resistance could result in death. Recovery was a sign that the chosen one had accepted the role of shaman and was prepared to undergo further initiation, which usually involved apprenticeship to a more experienced mediator with the spirit world. Such initiations and apprenticeships were generally prolonged, rigorous and complex. One mastered the properties of herbs and other substances used in healing and became adept in the rituals invoking the awesome power of procreation.

The ritual for the beaver bundle is long and difficult. There are more than three hundred songs to be learned before one can lead the ceremony of the beaver. In the bundle are the skins of beavers, otters, and many kinds of birds and water animals. With each of these there are songs, for each brought some power to the man who first saw it as a vision....At the planting and the gathering of the tobacco, the beaver bundle is opened and the ritual sung. The garden and the plants are sacred, for tobacco must be offered to all the powers of the earth, and of the water. A beaver man must keep count of the days, the moons and the winters. For this he keeps a set of sticks like those sometimes found in a beaver's house. At all times he must be ready to tell the moon and the day; he must say when it is time to go to the sun, moon, stars, winds and clouds so that he may know what the weather will be. If he is holy and good, he will have visions and dreams of power and so become a shaman.

When I first began to study the beaver medicine, I spent hours on the hilltops and near the waters, meditating and watching the birds, animals and the heavens.

—SMOKING-STAR, BLACKFOOT

*If a man is to do
something more than
human, he must have more
than human power.*

—TRADITIONAL

ost shamans possessed a medicine bundle — a collection of objects that were themselves endowed with supernatural powers, or the capacity to transmit them. Such bundles might include crystals, used for diagnosis, unusually marked or specially shaped stones; the feathers of sacred birds; and herbs or hallucinogenic substances. The sacred stones were often believed to have originated in the body of the medicine man himself.

Many native peoples had long-standing knowledge of herbal therapies and other forms of traditional healing.

O ye people, be ye healed;
Life anew I bring unto ye.
Through the Father over all
Do I thus.
Life anew I bring unto ye.

—GOOD EAGLE, DAKOTA SIOUX

Before seeking the aid of the shaman's magical medicine, they might appeal to healers and medicine societies for the treatment of common ailments, or those that might be cured by "suggestive" medicine, purifying sweat baths, or other approaches.

Treatment by shamans often took the form of ritualized extraction from the body of the substance that was believed to have caused the disease. This was done, both literally and symbolically, by pulling or sucking out the ailment, foreign substance, or evil spirit. Sometimes the cure also entailed recovery of the patient's dream soul, which was believed to have strayed from the owner's body, or to have been stolen by the dead.

Left: *The ephemeral Navajo sand painting, used in sacred Chantway healing rites and then destroyed to signify that the image has captured and overcome the patient's disharmony of body, mind, or spirit.*

Opposite: *Navajo sacred symbols depicted in this artwork based on elements of a sand painting include the corn plant, the turtle and the ancestral Holy People.*

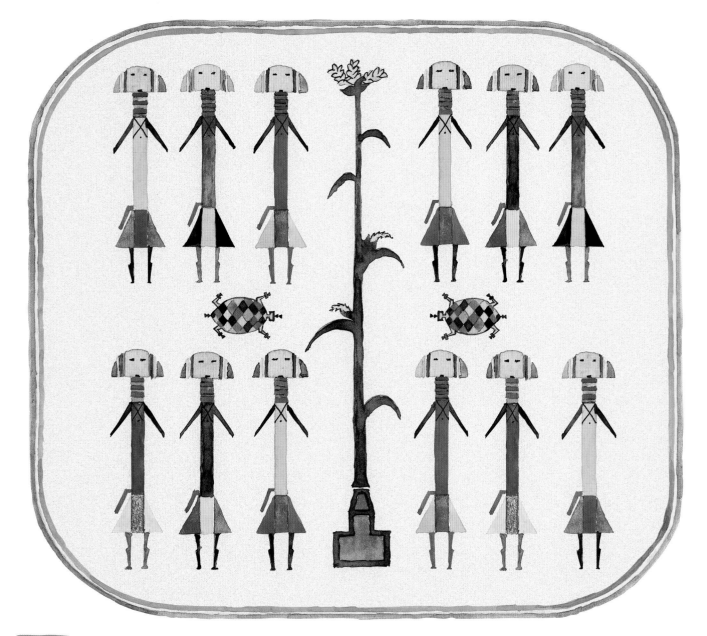

nother ritual form of healing was the sand painting ceremony, which was practiced among Southwestern peoples and developed to its height by the Navajo. Essentially, the Navajo sand painting is a temporary altar made on the floor of the ceremonial *hogan* by one or more artists skilled in the designs prescribed by the ancestral Holy People. The patient sits within the sacred image facing east, while the ritual singer performs the appropriate rites. Crushed colored stone, charcoal, ocher and other dry materials are used to create the "painting," which may include the symbols for Father Sky, Mother Earth, sacred springs, crop guardians, plants—all depicted according to one of hundreds of patterns transmitted by an ancestral chant hero. Blessings and offerings invoke the presence of the Holy People themselves, as the singer transfers sands from various parts of their images to the corresponding body parts of the afflicted person. Thus the sand painting is made and destroyed within the day, and its constituents returned to nature.

*Take your sacred pipe
and walk into their midst.
Have pity on your people
and love them.*

—WINNEBAGO

ometimes ritual knowledge could be passed on to practitioners who had no direct contact with spirit powers through dreams, visions, or spirit possession. These practitioners, whose functions resembled those of priests, acquired their knowledge through forms of apprenticeship to shamans and other priests. In several stratified agricultural societies, especially those of the Southeast and California, a kind of priestly caste supervised and performed the elaborate rituals marking the annual cycles. They also acted as the guardians of sacred temples and ceremonial sites and of sacred objects used in rituals and ceremonies.

Most shamans, however, learned their powers gradually and through what was essentially solitary meditation, usually beginning in childhood. Over time, the wisdom acquired from listening to their elders and seeking communion with spiritual powers would help the student to develop his own medicine and understanding.

By fasting and painting your face with ashes, you may get a blessing from the Manitou. If you do the right thing, you will surely be blessed. If you are afraid, the Manitou will know it….In the early days it was said that if one fasted long to obtain a blessing from the Manitou, he often went on the war-path successfully; or he killed people by fasting so long. Such was the blessing the person obtained. And you can go and kill game easily. You may become a leader in anything….All the people will be benefited by you.

—SAUK

Opposite: *An Inuit shamanic dance in the tradition of the Yupik of the coastal Bering Sea region.*

he shaman occupied the central place in the spiritual life of some groups of Inuit, among whom he was the sole mentor. He obtained his powers through contacts with various animal spirits in dreams. They taught him how to draw upon their power to cure disease and to divine the future. The pragmatic Inuit accepted a shaman on the basis of his success as a healer and visionary. Shamans were sometimes called upon to protect a community from evil spirits, or from an evil soul within it. Life was threatened by such malevolent supernatural powers and by the evil shamans who served them. The Inuit shaman was an ecstatic, capable of entering various states of spiritual possession and gifted with powers to control the weather, cure illnesses and locate lost persons or things.

You already possess everything necessary to become great.

—CROW PROVERB

Medicine Societies

Medicine societies were especially prevalent in the Northeast, among Iroquoian- and Algonquian-speaking peoples. Membership in these societies—determined sometimes by heredity, sometimes by election—generally included tribal leaders, those who had experienced a passage through disease, shamans, medicine men and visionaries. Assuming various complex forms, these associations met once or twice a year to conduct elaborate rituals, perform feats of magic and share esoteric knowledge. The Zuñi of the Southwest had an organization of twelve medicine societies under the sponsorship of the *wemaawe*, the "beast gods," of which the most important was the bear, whose image occurs on masks used in Zuñi healing ceremonies.

Members of the Iroquois medicine society (the False Face Society) wore carved masks while performing their rituals. These masks were revered as household gods, and regular offerings of food and tobacco were made to them.

There is no fear where there is faith.

—KIOWA PROVERB

The more you understand, the more you will trust and the less you will fear.

— MIDEWIWIN PRAYER, OJIBWA

According to the Ojibwa myth of the origins of the medicine society (the Midewiwin), it was Menabozho, a culture hero and intermediary between the Great Spirit and humankind, who gave the Midewiwin rituals to humans through the otter. The Ojibwa believed that these rituals were first performed to comfort Menabozho when his brother died. The Ojibwa medicine society had as many as 1,000 members, including all the tribal shamans and medicine men, and other persons of distinction who could purchase admission and undergo a four-step initiation process, of which the most important stage was the initiate's ritual death and rebirth into possession of powers of both healing and death-dealing. Other special powers focused on securing food and success in war.

It was the evening of the fourth day of the Midewiwin, or Medicine ceremony. The preceding three days and nights had been spent by the four masters, led by Terrible-eagle, in preparing Little-wolf within a room, formed by curtaining off one end of the lodge and in hanging the initiation fees, four sets of valuable goods — clothing, robes, weapons, copper utensils — on the ridge pole at the eastern end of the lodge; and in dedicating them.

As the sun set, the four old men and the candidate [for initiation] entered the lodge, followed by the men and women of the tribe who were already members of the society. Going in at the eastern door, the procession filed along the north side, and passing once regularly around, the people seated themselves on the right of the door, with the candidate on the west side of them, next to the Terrible-eagle.

— MENOMINEE

Left: *Iroquois corn-husk False Face dolls, emblems of the confederation's medicine society rites.*

Family and Community

All of this [world] is sacred, and so do not forget. Every dawn as it comes is a holy event, and every day is holy...and also you must always remember that the two-leggeds and all the other peoples who stand upon this earth are sacred and should be treated as such.

—WHITE BUFFALO CALF WOMAN

With all things and in all things, we are relatives.

—SIOUX PROVERB

The continent's first people have consistently advocated respect for all others who share the world, no matter how different their lifeways. Yet despite this fellow-feeling with the wider community of humankind, their identity is closely bound up with the ties of family, tribe and clan. All aspects of family and tribal tradition, spiritual beliefs and the skills essential to daily life are passed down the generations through a continuous cycle in which children learn by imitating and listening to their elders—parents, grandparents and tribal or clan wise people. Thus, the family is the source of wisdom, learning and a profound sense of cultural belonging as well as an individual's emotional homeplace. Chief Joseph recalled:

Our fathers gave us many laws, which they had learned from their fathers. These laws were good. They told us to treat all people as they treated us; that we should never be the first to break a bargain; that it was a disgrace to tell a lie; that we should speak only the truth.

—CHIEF JOSEPH, NEZ PERCÉ

Opposite: Singer for the Clan, *by artist Jesse Hummingbird, is a vivid contemporary image of a member of the Deer Clan who sings its stories from memory for the community.*

Overleaf: Inuit hunters in kayaks surround a member of the Ford-Bartlett expedition to East Greenland, which excavated native sites at Angmagssalik.

Previous pages: The sacred rock formation known as the Corn Twins, near the Hopi burial ground at Walpi, Arizona.

In traditional native communities, family and clan identity were intimately connected to the homeplace, the place where earlier generations had lived and were buried, their spirits often called upon for guidance. Plenty Coups, a Crow chief, said: "The ground on which we stand is sacred ground. It is the dust and blood of our ancestors."

The common bonds of tribal heritage and love for a shared homeplace foster a sense of unity within clans and groups. From an early age, children learn to regard their kin with a respect and affection that deepen with each passing year. In the words of the Crow elder Shining Arrows, "If you have one hundred people who live together, and if each one cares for the rest, there is One Mind."

Working together makes each man's task simpler.

— CREE SAYING

Responsibility and respect—for elders, contemporaries and children, for past and future generations—bring a sense of the continuity of life, and the concept that all is one and eternally renewed. From this perspective, life is less about conquest than it is about stewardship. In the words of Anna L. Walters, Pawnee: "Everything changes, and yet nothing changes but the holders of life. In the Great Mystery, it is unending." A Salish elder underlines the role of love in this oration:

Love is something you and I must have. We must have it because our spirit feeds upon it. We must have it because without it we become weak and faint. Without love our self-esteem weakens. Without it our courage fails. Without love we can no longer look out confidently at the world. We turn inward and begin to feed upon our own personalities, and little by little we destroy ourselves.

With it we are creative. With it we march tirelessly. With it, and with it alone, we are able to sacrifice for others.

—CHIEF DAN GEORGE, SALISH

Left: *Cherokee artist Jeanne Walker Rorex captures the essence of maternity in her evocative 1989 painting* Contented Hands.

The Woman's Way

Woman is forever, eternal. Man comes from woman and to woman he returns.

— OJIBWA SAYING

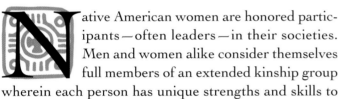

Native American women are honored participants—often leaders—in their societies. Men and women alike consider themselves full members of an extended kinship group wherein each person has unique strengths and skills to contribute to the common well-being.

In traditional Native American communities, women's powers of generativity identified them with Mother Earth, and spiritual power was perceived in the cycles of puberty, sexual union, pregnancy, childbirth and nursing. According to Ohiyesa (Charles Eastman), the renowned physician, writer and activist:

> *From the moment of the mother's recognition that she had conceived to the end of the child's second year of life, which was the ordinary duration of lactation, it was supposed by us that the mother's spiritual influence was supremely important.*
>
> *Her attitude and secret meditations must be such as to instill into the receptive soul of the unborn child the love of the Great Mystery and a sense of connectedness with all creation. Silence and isolation are the rule of life for the expectant mother.*
>
> OHIYESA, SANTEE SIOUX

In most native communities, both menarche and childbirth were surrounded by various rituals and taboos designed to protect the power that attended the capacity to give and sustain life. Sequestration at these times did not imply uncleanness, but respect. In some tribes, women gave birth alone in a designated shelter, or in the woods. In others, older women of the community acted as midwives and spirit helpers and assisted the new mother and the baby in its first days of life. Fathers, as in some California tribes, might assume the mother's usual tasks of drawing water and collecting firewood during late pregnancy and confinement.

omen of the immediate family and clan were usually responsible for child care during the child's early years, after which the father and uncles took over the education of sons in the ways of male roles within their community. Girls remained with their mothers to learn healing, agricultural and domestic duties—which often included the maintenance of the family dwelling. Grandparents and other elders played vital roles, as described by Lakota chief Luther Standing Bear:

Our young people, raised under the old rules of courtesy, never indulge in the present habit of talking incessantly and all at the same time. To do so would have been not only impolite, but foolish; for poise, so much admired as a social grace, could not be accompanied by restlessness. Pauses were acknowledged gracefully and did not cause lack of ease or embarrassment.

In talking to children, the old Lakota would place a hand on the ground and explain: "We sit in the lap of our Mother. From her we, and all other living things, come. We shall soon pass, but the place where we now rest will last forever." So we, too, learned to sit or lie on the ground and become conscious of life about us in its multitude of forms.

—LUTHER STANDING BEAR, LAKOTA

We sit in the lap of our Mother. From her we, and all other living things, come.
—LUTHER STANDING BEAR, LAKOTA

Right: Cooking Fry Bread shows three generations of artist Norma Howard's family (Mississippi Choctaw/Chickasaw):

"Grandma told stories to my sisters and me," she recalls from her childhood, *"as my mother and aunt prepared fry bread."*

Care for your garden like you care for your children, to nurture health, strength and growth.

— IROQUOIS SAYING

Among their families and clans, women passed on their knowledge of herbs and other plants to their daughters. At inter-tribal gatherings, they exchanged seeds, which were taken into new regions for cultivation. Some 2,000 years ago, sunflowers, marsh elder, goosefoot and herbs were grown. At first, the plots cleared by fire and tended with stick tools were modest, and survival depended mainly on the pre-agricultural food sources from gathering, hunting and fishing. Gradually, women's understanding of the earth, their crops and the local climate deepened, and agriculture became a sustainable way of life for many tribes.

In the Southwest, the Pueblo peoples have cultivated maize, or corn, from ancient times. Zuñi legend attrib-uted this great gift to the Six Corn Maidens, who transformed the native grasses into their staple food. Women cultivated, dried, stored and ground the sacred crop.

The importance of their plantations as reliable food sources grew and spread. Women of the Eastern woodlands introduced the cultivation of "the three sisters"—corn, beans and squash—as companion crops that supported ever larger and more stable communities. Their other tasks were also essential to the community. Depending upon the regions they inhabited, women built shelters of birch bark, brush, hide and adobe; fashioned baskets and pottery; drew and carried water; prepared hides and fur for use as clothing; cared for the tribe's livestock; gathered acorns, roots and berries; and did the myriad household tasks of women everywhere.

Right: *A Mahican woman prepares food in this scene from a mural by Olin Dow in the post office at Rhinebeck, New York.*

Childhood

Remember that your children are not your own, but are lent to you by the Creator.

—MOHAWK PROVERB

Opposite: *A young child remains under the watchful eye of his mother as she collects water, photographed by Edward Curtis.*

Below: *Stringing chili peppers to dry at San Ildefonso Pueblo — a cooperative task, as photographed by T. Harmon Parkhurst.*

Childhood training began early as a part of play. Young boys were given small bows with untipped arrows and earned larger bows as they grew older. They learned how to stalk game, to hit moving targets and to fight. Their stalking games, archery matches and mock battles were competitive, the winners earning warm praise from fathers and elders. Smoking-Star, a Blackfoot shaman, recalled from his boyhood:

When [I was] about six years old one of my grandfathers made me a bow; he prayed for me and said if I killed anything I should bring in the scalp to prove it. He told me the story of Scar-face and the dangerous birds. Some time after this I killed a bird, my first, and my father made a feast, calling in many great men, who smoked pipes, told of great deeds and predicted that I would be a great warrior. The skin of the bird was put into my grandfather's war bundle.

—SMOKING-STAR, BLACKFOOT

irls were taught how to grow and prepare food, identify herbs and plants, maintain the family dwelling and other traditional skills. by example from their mothers, sisters and grandmothers. In this account of an Iroquois childhood:

The summers passed, and Hanging-flower was a baby no longer. Her mother taught her the art of cooking; she also began to help when the corn was pounded in large, wooden mortars. Soon she learned how to embroider. And as her fingers grew nimble and her eyes fond of the colored beads and wampum shells, she began to feel that the world of buds and flowers and leaves was her own, hers and her mother's and of the other women; — the men knew nothing of such things.

— IROQUOIS

Great Plains girls learned to sew by making clothing for their dolls from scraps of hide and were given miniature tipis to set up in emulation of their mothers. In the Great Basin, children participated in food-gathering at an early age and enjoyed almost unrestricted freedom of activity. In the Southwest, girls learned from their mothers how to nurture and prepare maize, as described in this memoir of early life in Oraibi, Arizona:

There was love in my home, and I felt happy and secure during my childhood. I began learning about life just like all children do, from imitating my elders. My mother seemed to be grinding corn most of the time. Little girls all over the village played at grinding corn. When I was about five years old my mother put me on a real grinding stone alongside her, with a few kernels of corn, and let me grind a little while. This corn, my initial grindings, she fed to the chickens.

— HELEN SEKAQUAPTEWA, HOPI

Love your children: They are your future.

— HOPI SAYING

Opposite: *A compelling portrait of mother and child at Jémez Pueblo about 1912.*

Left: *A reluctant young Arapaho sitter poses with miniature cradleboard during a Curtis tour of the Great Plains.*

Overleaf: *A shy Inuit child carries her sled-dog pup nestled in her parka (left); A Hopi elder dresses an adolescent girl's hair in the traditional whorls that proclaim her coming of age as a woman of marriageable status (right).*

*It takes a whole village
to raise a child.*

—OMAHA PROVERB

As children matured, restrictions were removed and special privileges were granted. A Blackfoot boy who won an archery match was allowed to place feathers in his hair like the older men. Among the Cheyenne, boys returning from their first war party were relieved of their usual duty of herding the horses.

Most native children learned informally through the example of their elders. Those who were removed to distant "Indian schools" established by the government usually suffered deeply. There, given new English names; forbidden to speak their own languages; dressed in uncomfortable, restrictive uniforms; confined indoors most of the time; and punished harshly for infractions of incomprehensible rules, they often sickened, and some died. Native parents, in turn, were extremely resistant to separating from their children and handing them over to foreign teachers and missionaries. This conflict endured for several centuries and became most prevalent during the early decades of the reservation era. Only in the fairly recent past has it become possible for a Native American spokesman to state with conviction:

I am glad our children are learning to read and write English, but I'm also very glad they're learning about the Navajo culture and the Navajo way. We want our children to be proud that they are Navajo.

— ROBERT A. ROESSEL, JR., NAVAJO

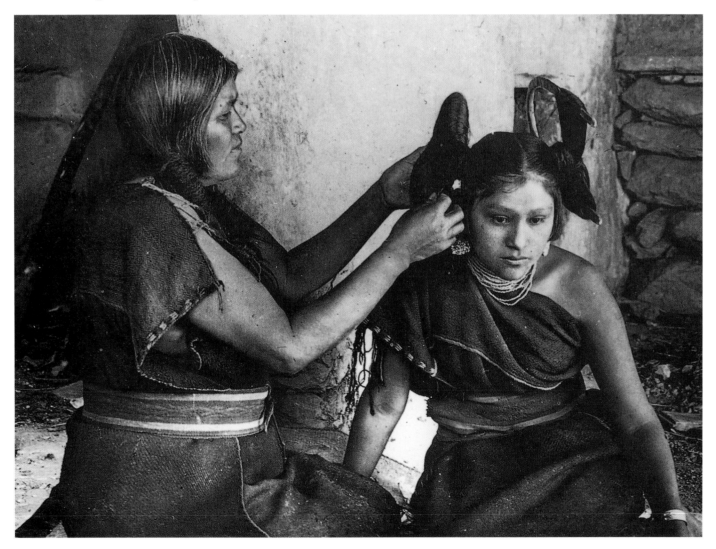

Learning the Man's Way

Young men experienced various rites of passage on their path to full maturity as hunters, warriors, fathers and, eventually, respected elders. Like the daughters of the tribe, they learned by example from an early age those skills that would contribute food, protection, spiritual harmony and other necessities for the common good. Responsible parenting was modeled by their male relatives—not only their fathers, but uncles, cousins, medicine men and bearers of the wisdom traditions. In the words of the Kapiosa Sioux Leaf Dweller: "If you are to be a leader…you must listen in silence to the mystery of the spirit."

Young men prided themselves on faithful adherence to the mores of their people, and personal bravery and integrity were highly esteemed. One might demonstrate these qualities through a vision quest, grueling rituals like the Plains Sun Dance, great powers of memory in preserving and transmitting oral tradition, prowess in combat and many other ways.

If shame was incurred by cowardice, treaty-breaking, greed, or other behavior inimical to the common good, this reflected upon the whole tribe or kinship group. Perseverance in the face of hunger, cold, an enemy superior in

You shall soon glory in the strength of your manhood, and your enemies afar shall hear your name and tremble.

—METHOATASKE
(MOTHER OF TECUMSEH), MUSCOGEE

> *The contrary winds may blow strong in my face,*
> *yet I will go forward and never turn back.*
>
> —TEEDYUSCUNG, LENAPE

numbers and other adversities brought honor. As a contemporary member of the Northwestern Coast Salish, Duane Niatum, has expressed it: "I protect my Klallam tribe and the Coast Salish path because my good name is a measure of its language and its arts."

In the Pueblo culture area, sacred songs and rituals were carried out by male initiates in underground kivas, or ceremonial chambers, and in the seasonal Antelope and Snake Dances. Members of the Iroquois League carved the sacred basswood masks of the False Face Society, and Inuit shamans defied the power of evil spirits and disease in their ecstatic rituals. In Native America, to this day:

> *It is the responsibility of the tribe to teach its children about*
> *their connection with the ancestors and to establish their*
> *place of inclusion in the circle of their Nation.*
>
> —E.K. COLDWELL, CHEROKEE/SHAWNEE

Right: *Members of the Northwestern Kwakiutl tribe bring a young woman promised in marriage to her new clan in a famous photograph by Curtis.*

Opposite: Buffalo Dancer *delineates the strength and purpose of a young Plainsman assuming his role in tribal ritual.*

The Wisdom of the Elders

I n Native America, old age and death are seen as aspects of the great cycle of life and are not deplored and feared. Age brings wisdom, which is revered, and elders play a major part in community life even when they can no longer hunt, plant, or gather:

Old age was simply a delightful time, when the old people sat on the sunny doorsteps, playing in the sun with the children, until they fell asleep. As last, they failed to wake up.
— JAMES PAYTIAMO, ACOMA PUEBLO

Hold fast to the words of your ancestors.

— HOPI PROVERB

Below: *A Nakoaktok craftswoman (left); The Blackfoot warrior Fat Horse (right).*

Opposite: *Oglala Sioux funeral rite near Fort Laramie, Wyoming.*

After death, the deceased was honored in a funeral rite, sometimes buried or, in other traditions, raised above ground to rest on a platform to prepare the soul for the next life. The body was given back to nature, whence it had come. An Ojibwa spokesman described his people's burial customs and the belief in an afterlife which was so prevalent in tribal cultures across the continent. It reflected the conviction that life was changed, not ended, by death:

When [one of us] dies, his body is placed in a grave, generally in a sitting posture, facing the west. With the body are buried all the articles needed in life for a journey. If a man, his gun, blanket, kettle, fire steel, flint, and moccasins; if a woman, her moccasins, ax, portage collar, blanket, and kettle. The soul is supposed to start immediately after the death of the body on a deep beaten path, which leads westward; the first object he comes to, in following this path, is the great Oda-e-min *(Heart Berry), or strawberry, which*

stands on the roadside like a huge rock, and from which he takes a handful and eats on his way. He travels on till he reaches a deep, rapid stream of water, over which lies the much-dreaded Ko-go-gaup-o-gun, *or rolling and sinking bridge; once safely over this, as the traveler looks back, it assumes the shape of a huge serpent twisting and untwisting its folds across the stream.*

After camping out four nights, and traveling each day through a prairie country, the soul arrives in the land of spirits, where he finds his relatives accumulated since mankind was first created; all is rejoicing, singing and dancing; they live in a beautiful country interspersed with clear lakes and streams, forests and prairies, and abounding in fruit and game to repletion—in a word, abounding in all that the red man most covets in this life, and which conduces most to his happiness. It is this kind of paradise which he only, by his manner of life on this earth, is fitted to enjoy.

—OJIBWA

The tribal elders figure in many legends, including the Choctaw creation story, which centers upon the great platform mound called Nunih Waya, in present-day Mississippi. This Great Mother of the Choctaw came to be as the people wandered in search of a homeland, carrying with them the bones of their revered ancestors. When they reached the destined place, they piled high the remains of their elders and covered them with cypress bark to create the sacred mound. Here they planted many trees and performed the renewal rite called the Green Corn Dance, at which they sang: "Look upon the great mound;…it inhumes the bones of fathers and relatives; they died on our sojourn in the wilderness. They died in a far-off wild country. They rest at Nunih Waya."

As Native Americans dwindled in numbers and power during the nineteenth and twentieth centuries, their lifeways inexorably eroded or destroyed in the post-contact clash of cultures, the elders expressed their grief in poignant prayers and recollections. In the words of the Hidatsa Waheenee:

I am an old woman now. The buffaloes and blacktail deer are gone, and our Indian ways are almost gone. Sometimes

I find it hard to believe that I ever lived them.

Often in summer I rise at daybreak and steal out to the cornfields, and as I hoe the corn I sing to it, as we did when I was young.

Sometimes in the evening I sit, looking out on the big Missouri. The sun sets, and dusk steals over the water. In the shadows I seem again to see our Indian village, with smoke curling upward from the earth lodges, and in the river's roar I hear the yells of the warriors, and the laughter of little children as of old. It is but an old woman's dream. Then I see but shadows and hear only the roar of the river, and tears come into my eyes.

—WAHEENEE, HIDATSA

The revered Lakota leader Black Elk voiced his last hope in the emotional prayer:

Again, and maybe the last time on this earth, I recall the great vision you sent me. It may be that some little root of the sacred tree still lives. Nourish it then, that it may leaf and bloom and fill with singing birds. Hear me, not for myself, but for my people; I am old. Hear me that they may once more go back into the sacred hoop and find the good red road, the shielding tree.

—BLACK ELK, OGLALA LAKOTA

A hundred years later, the contemporary Cherokee/Creek elder Glenn J. Twist would reflect on his role in the life of his people:

I am a storyteller....I am the last generation of my family to be born in the Boston Mountains of Arkansas and Oklahoma, as well as on a Cherokee allotment. If I don't preserve the stories I've heard, they will be lost forever.

—GLENN J. TWIST, CHEROKEE/CREEK

I am one hundred and one, and I know that sometimes many paths go to the same place.

—WHITE CALF, PIEGAN/BLACKFOOT

Left: *Big Foot's band of Minneconjou Lakota gather for the Grass Dance along South Dakota's Cheyenne River in 1890.*

A Common Destiny

Native Americans have traditionally defined themselves in the context of a higher good: that of the community. While individual responsibility is important, a person's actions always have repercussions for the community at large: One person's humiliation brings shame or bad medicine upon the tribe or band, and a good deed reaps rewards for all. Many tasks are undertaken communally, like hunting and preparing animal hides. All families participate in celebrations and rituals, and the sense of community is inextricably linked with the homeplace. As the Sauk leader Black Hawk described it:

We always had plenty; our children never cried from hunger; neither were our people in want….The rapids of Rock River furnished us with an abundance of excellent fish, and the land, being very fertile, never failed to produce good crops of corn, beans, pumpkins and squashes….Here our village stood for more than one hundred years, during all of which time we were the undisputed possessors of the Mississippi Valley….Our village was healthy and there was no place in the country possessing such advantages, nor hunting grounds better than those we had in possession.

— BLACK HAWK, SAUK

The founder of the powerful Iroquois League, known as the Peacemaker, advocated mutual esteem among members of the confederation and respect for other peoples as well, advising: "Listen, that the peace may continue unto future days!" And the renowned Shawnee/Muscogee leader Tecumseh, who sought to unite disparate tribes in the face of Euroamerican encroachment, recommended that his people "Show respect for all men, but grovel to none." To this day, as Oglala Lakota Arthur L. McDonald has observed: "The traditional Indian culture…has as its ultimate good the survival of the tribe."

Opposite: *A Curtis photograph of Absaroke hunters in the mountains of the northern Plains.*

Left: *Arapaho women peg down a hide for tanning, a traditionally communal task, at the Wind River Reservation.*

Through these groves and over these prairies in pursuit of game our fathers roamed, and by them this land was left to us as a heritage forever.

— SENACHWINE, POTOWATOMI

n times of adversity, the importance of uniting against threats and opponents becomes even greater. The redoubtable resistance leader Goyathlay, (Geronimo) spent most of his life fighting to defend the Southwestern homelands of his people:

For each tribe…Usen created, He also made a home. In the land for any particular tribe He placed whatever would be best for the welfare of that tribe.
— GERONIMO, CHIRICAHUA APACHE

Among the most moving testimonies to the spiritual solidarity of Native American kinship is the unforgettable eulogy to the Nez Percé way of life voiced by the defeated Chief Joseph after his 1,500-mile running battle with the U.S. Army. Deprived of their ancestral lands in Oregon's Wallowa Valley, the Nez Percé sought to escape to Canada from an Idaho reservation, but were stopped just short of their goal at Bear Paw Mountain, Montana. Joseph dismounted and thrust his rifle into the hands of General Miles Howard with the words:

I am tired of fighting….The old men are all dead….The little children are freezing to death. My people, some of them, have run away to the hills and have no blankets, no food. No one knows where they are….
Hear me, my chiefs! I am tired; my heart is sick and sad. From where the sun now stands, I will fight no more forever.
— CHIEF JOSEPH, NEZ PERCÉ

Despite all adversities, the wisdom of the elders of hundreds of nations has survived in both oral and, more recently, written tradition to enrich the cultural heritage of the continent. The contemporary renaissance of Native American pride and identity, manifested in activism, education, art and literature, has dispelled many of the myths created by generations of revisionist history, opening the way to an ever-wider appreciation of indigenous cultures and their profound wisdom traditions.

The Potowatomi elder New Corn expressed his people's conviction in the words: "I am old, but I shall never die. I shall always live in my children, and children's children." In this way, the unbroken circle of life continues, and the wisdom of countless generations endures in those who celebrate anew the sacred in everyday life.

We shall live again;
We shall live again.
— GHOST DANCE SONG, COMANCHE

Left: *Paiute activist Sarah Winnemucca.*

Opposite: Her Heart's Strength: On the Trail of Tears, *by Jeanne Walker Rorex.*

Index

Page numbers in **boldface** refer to illustrations.

Bibliography and Sources

Alexander, Hartley B., 1916. *North American Mythology.* (*The Mythology of All Races in Thirteen Volumes*, Vol. X, ed. Louis H. Gray, Boston: Marshal Jones Company.

Benedict, Ruth, 1922. "The Vision in Plains Culture," *American Anthropologist* (New Series), XXIV, 1-23.

———, 1976. *Myths and Tales of the American Indians.* New York: Indian Head Books.

Boas, Franz, 1915. "Mythology and Folk-tales of the North American Indians," Franz Boas et al. *Anthropology in North America.* New York: G.E. Stechert, pp. 306–349.

Burland, Cottie, revised by Wood, Marion, 1985. *North American Indian Mythology.* New York: Peter Bedrick Books.

Capps, Walter Holden, editor, 1976. *Seeing with a Native Eye.* New York: Harper & Row.

Catlin, George, 1841. *The Manners, Customs and Conditions of the North American Indians.* London. 2 volumes, reprinted 1973, New York: Dover.

Cleary, Kristen Marée, editor, 1996. *Native American Wisdom.* New York: Barnes & Noble, Inc.

Collier, John, 1947. *Indians of the Americas — The Long Hope.* New York, W.W. Norton & Co.

Curtis, Nathalie, 1923. *The Indians' Book: Songs and Legends of the Indians.* Reprint, 1968, New York: Dover Publications.

Deloria, Vine, Jr., 1973. *God is Red.* New York: Dell Publications.

Dooling, J.M. & Jordan-Smith, P., editors, 1989. *I Become Part of It — Sacred Dimensions in Native American Life.* New York: Parabola.

Dozier, E.P., 1970. *The Pueblo Indians of North America.* New York: Holt, Rinehart and Winston.

Eastman, Charles A., 1911. *The Soul of an Indian.* Boston: Houghton Mifflin Company.

Fire, John (Lame Deer) and Erdoes, Richard, 1972. *Lame Deer, Seeker of Visions.* New York: Simon & Schuster.

Gill, Sam D. & Sullivan, Irene F., 1992. *Dictionary of Native American Mythology.* Oxford: ABC-CLIO.

Grinnell, George B., 1920. *Blackfoot Lodge Tales.* New York.

———, 1889. *Pawnee Hero Stories and Folk-Tales.* New York: Forest and Stream Publishing Company. Paperback reprint, Lincoln: University of Nebraska Press, 1961.

Hassrick, Royal B., 1964. *The Sioux, Life and Customs of a Warrior Society.* Norman, University of Oklahoma Press.

Hyemeyohsts, Storm, 1972. *Seven Arrows.* New York: Ballantine Books.

Hertzberg, Hazel W., 1971. *The Search for an American Indian Identity, Modern Pan-Indian Movements.* Syracuse: Syracuse University Press.

Jorgensen, Joseph G., 1972. *The Sun Dance Religion, Power for the Powerless.* Chicago: University of Chicago Press.

La Barre, W., 1938. *The Peyote Cult.* (Yale University Publications in Anthropology, 19) New Haven.

———, 1970. *The Ghost Dance. Origins of Religion.* Garden City, N.Y.: Doubleday.

Lowie, Robert H., 1915, *The Sun Dance of the Crow Indians.* New York: Anthropological Papers of the American Museum of Natural History, (16) 1, pp. 1–50.

McLuhan, T.C., 1971. *Touch the Earth, A Self-Portrait of Indian Existence.* New York: Outerbridge & Dienstfrey.

Miller, David H., 1959, *Ghost Dance.* New York: Duell, Sloan and Pearce.

Miller, Lee, editor, 1995. *From the Heart: Voices of the American Indian.* New York: Alfred A. Knopf.

Mooney, James, 1896, "The Ghost Dance Religion and the Sioux Outbreak of 1890," *14th Annual Report of the Bureau of Ethnology, Part 1.* Washington, D.C.: Government Printing Office, pp. 3–548

Nabokov, Peter, editor, 1991. *Native American Testimony: A Chronicle of Indian-White Relations from Prophecy to the Present, 1492–1992.* New York: Viking Penguin.

Neihardt, John, 1932. *Black Elk Speaks.* New York.

Opler, Morris. E., 1941. *An Apache Life-Way.* Chicago: University of Chicago Press.

Parsons, Elsie C., 1922. *North American Indian Life.* New York: B.W. Huebsch.

Radin, Paul, 1914. "Religion of the North American Indians," *Journal of American Folk-Lore,* XXVII, 335–73.

Regier, Willis G., editor, 1993. *Masterpieces of American Indian Literature.* New York, MJF Books.

Spier, Leslie, 1921. *The Sun Dance of the Plains Indians: Its Development and Diffusion.* (Anthropological Papers of the American Museum of Natural History, Vol. XVI, Part 7) New York.

Steiner, Stan, 1968. *The New Indians.* New York.

Tedlock, Dennis & Barbara, 1975. *Teachings from the American Earth, Indian Religion and Philosophy.* New York: Liveright.

Thompson, Stith, 1929. *Tales of the North American Indians.* Cambridge, Massachusetts: Harvard University Press.

Turner, Frederick, editor, 1973. *The Portable North American Reader.* New York: The Viking Press.

Udall, Louise, 1969. *Me and Mine: The Life Story of Helen Sekaquaptewa.* Arizona: University of Arizona Press.

Underhill, Ruth M., 1953. *Red Man's America.* Chicago: University of Chicago Press.

Waters, Frank, 1963. *Book of the Hopi.* New York: The Viking Press.

Zona, Guy A., 1994. *The Soul Would Have No Rainbow if the Eyes Had No Tears.* New York: Simon & Schuster Inc.

Acknowledgements and Picture Credits

The publisher would like to thank the following individuals for their assistance in the preparation of this book: Sara Hunt, editor; John Letterman, Marie Whitla O'Reilly and Robin Langley Sommer, contributing editors; Nicola J. Gillies, managing editor; Charles J. Ziga, art director; Lisa Desautels, indexer. Grateful acknowledgement is also made to the individuals and institutions listed below for permission to reproduce artwork and photographs:

Artists: ©**Norma Howard**: 90–91; ©**Jesse Hummingbird**: 10, 17, 85; ©**Keith Hunt**: front jacket artwork, 1, 2, 5, 77; ©**Barthell Little Chief**: 18–19, 33; ©**Jeanne Walker Rorex**: 35, 88. *Photography*: ©**Corel Inc**: 26; ©**Glenn O. Myers**: 6–7, 14–15, 28–29, 50–51, 54–55, 56–57, 82–83; ©**Lorraine B. Myers**: 75; ©**Jay Olstad**: 68, 92; ©**Michael Tincher**: 23, 76; ©**Jack Vartoogian**: 79; ©**Charles J. Ziga**: 20–21, 27, 64, 65; © Charles J. Ziga, collection of Glenn O. and Lorraine B. Myers: 22, 80 (both), 81. *Historical images:* Collection of Frank Oppel: 8–9, 69; Library of Congress, Prints and Photographs Division: 30–31, 34, 37, 39, 45, 47, 59, 60, 62l, 63, 69, 70, 71, 72, 86–87, 95, 96, 100, 101, 102 (both), 107; Museum of New Mexico: 93, 94, 97; National Archives of Canada: 11, 53b, 98; Nebraska State Historical Society: 12, 104–05; Northwind Photo Archive, hand colored by Nancy Carter: 108; Saraband Image Library: 38, 42, 43, 44, 46, 52, 53t, 58, 61, 62r, 74, 78, 84, 89, 92; State Historical Society of Wyoming, Division of Cultural Resources: 106.